The New Stations

of the Cross

Also by Megan McKenna

Not Counting Women and Children: Neglected Stories from the Bible

Leave Her Alone

*Blessings and Woes: The Beatitudes and the Sermon on the Plain
in the Gospel of Luke*

Dancing With Angels: Selected Poems

Rites of Justice: The Sacraments and Liturgy As Ethical Imperatives

Keepers of the Story: Oral Traditions in Religion

Parables: The Arrows of God

Angels Unawares

Mary: Shadow of Grace

Lent: The Sunday Readings

Lent: The Daily Readings, Reflections, and Stories

Mary, Mother of All Nations

Prophets: Words of Fire

Marrow of Mystery: Selected Poems

Justice Charity Community: Our Trinity on Earth (audio)

Advent, Christmas, Epiphany

*Advent, Christmas, and Epiphany: Stories and Reflections on the
Daily Readings*

Christ All Merciful

The New Stations of the Cross

■

The Way of the Cross
According to Scripture

■

Megan McKenna

IMAGE BOOKS

DOUBLEDAY

New York   London   Toronto   Sydney   Auckland

for Aidan, wayfaring friend, with grateful love

AN IMAGE BOOK
PUBLISHED BY DOUBLEDAY
a division of Random House, Inc.
IMAGE, DOUBLEDAY and the portrayal of a deer drinking from a stream are
registered trademarks of Random House, Inc.

Library of Congress Cataloging-in-Publication Data

McKenna, Megan.
The new Stations of the Cross : the Way of the Cross according to Scripture /
by Megan McKenna.—1st Image Books ed.
p. cm.
Includes bibliographical references.
1. Stations of the Cross. I. Title.

BX2040 .M36 2003
232.96—dc21
2002027351

ISBN 0-385-50815-8

February 2003

First Image Books Edition

1   3   5   7   9   10   8   6   4   2

Contents

Introduction

Come, O Faithful, let us bow before the lifegiving cross on which
Christ, the King of Glory, freely stretched out his hands.
. . . Filled with fear and awe, we embrace you,
We glorify our God and we say: O Lord, you were nailed on the cross;
in your goodness and love, have mercy on us.

—FROM ANCIENT BYZANTINE HYMN, SUNG AT VESPERS
FOR THE FEAST OF THE ELEVATION OF THE HOLY CROSS,
SEPTEMBER 14, ORIGINAL CHURCH SLAVONIC

The devotion of the Way of the Cross, or the Stations of the Cross, goes back to the earliest centuries of the church. Many people wanted to walk the land where Jesus lived and trace his path from the Garden of Olives to the High Priest's house and courtyard, then on to Pilate's residence and the Praetorium, through the city of Jerusalem and outside to the hill of Calvary, the garbage dump outside the city, and then at last to the tomb in a garden. Yet many couldn't get to Jerusalem, or if they could, only once in their lifetime on pilgrimage. They desired to follow literally in the footsteps of their Crucified Master and Risen Lord, stopping along the way to reflect on his life, on his sufferings, and his death by crucifixion. This led to the ritual devotion of walking the Way of the Cross based on the Scriptures.

Over time, depending upon who designed the devotion, pieces were added that were not in the Scriptures but they wanted them to be. Veronica added herself, it is thought, as part of the devotional practice. Christians found it difficult to stand up to evil and resist sin, so they added the three stations of Jesus falling, though the Bible does not record that he did so. And because of great devotion to the Mother of God, they added a station where the two, mother and son, met and another where she held his lifeless body in her arms before putting him into the tomb. This image, of course, became the pietà.

These images were added to the ritual because of popular piety, because of their emotional content, and because of ignorance of the Scriptures, especially in the Middle Ages, when reading the Scriptures was often relegated to houses of study and monasteries. Many other stations were added as well, sometimes totaling twenty or more, as the faithful sought ways to personalize and experience the way Jesus walked on the earth, especially during the season of Lent and Holy Week.

Over a decade ago, Pope John Paul II decided to alter the traditional fourteen stations, dropping out the ones that were not in the Scriptures and adding other portions from the gospel accounts. Part of the simple introduction stated, "The following stations of the cross are based on those celebrated by Pope John Paul II on Good Friday 1991. They are presented here as an alternative to the traditional stations and as a way of reflecting more deeply on the Scriptural accounts of Christ's passion." Since then, on Good Friday, the Pope has sometimes selected alternative accounts from other gospels. These choices are what this book and its reflections are based upon. This past year, 2002, the Pope requested that eleven reporters write portions of the reflections because he wanted to emphasize and highlight the extreme importance of the media and show how the stations were not just about the Way of the Cross that Jesus trod in his passion, but about the Way of the Cross that all believers, especially those who suffer violently, innocently, needlessly, and in the cause of justice, still walk in their passion in contemporary society. This devotion is not so much about the past as about the present reality of the Crucified One in our midst still suffering and dying at our hands.

This emphasis on scriptural content seems to us in this century to be something new, but it was the bedrock and core of the first five hundred years of the Church. Listen to some of the comments of great writers.

> Just as at the sea those who are carried away from the direction of the harbor bring themselves back on course by a clear sign, on seeing a tall beacon light or some mountain peak coming into view, so Scripture may guide those adrift on the sea of life back into the harbor of the divine will.
>
> (GREGORY OF NYSSA)

> Everything we read in the sacred Books shines and glitters even in the outer shell; but the marrow is sweeter. He who desires to eat the kernel must first break open the shell.
>
> (JEROME)

> Learn to fix the eye of faith on the divine word of the Holy Scriptures as on a light shining place until the day dawn and the day-star arise in your hearts. For the ineffable source from which this lamp borrows its light is the Light that shines in the darkness but the darkness does not comprehend it. To see it, our hearts must be purified by faith.
>
> (AUGUSTINE OF HIPPO)

Once again the Scriptures are a lodestar, a benchmark, the plumb line that steadies us and steers us clear of what is happening in the world and gives us a glimpse of history and politics, economics and daily experiences from God's point of view. Going back to this mother lode of wisdom and knowledge, inspired by God, brings grace and further insight not found in other devotional materials. In these words of God we find a lifeline and a compass for venturing into the world as believers, walking with Jesus, the Crucified and Risen One. But this immersion in Scripture and amending devotions and practices to adhere more closely to the Scriptures has effects that we may be unaware of initially. The monk Thomas Merton wrote this of the Word of God and what it could do to those who read it and sought to put it into practice:

> Any serious reading of the Bible means personal involvement in it, not simple mental agreement with abstract propositions. And involvement is dangerous, because it lays one open to unforeseen conclusions.

These powerful readings, coupled with contemporary accounts of the world's suffering and pain, invite us to a large way of the cross, crisscrossing along the earth's face, crossing borders and nationalities, cultures and languages, economic and social lines. But always the stories and the pain are the same, the characters are those of the gospels of Mark, Matthew, Luke, and John. The struggles for integrity, courage in the face of evil, humanity in the face of what horror human beings inflict upon each other, and justice and peace as antidotes to the curse of injustice and war, all these are the common inheritance of those who believe and follow after their Lord, Jesus the Crucified One. As the Latin American writer and historian Eduardo Galeano writes, "Today we must begin again. Step by small step, without any more protection than comes from our own bodies." Or as Karol Wojtyla wrote before becoming John Paul II, "I am a wayfarer on the narrow pavement of earth and I do not put aside the thought of Your face, which the world does not reveal to me." The walking of the Way of the Cross is the lifestyle of Christians, celebrated ritually in the Stations of the Cross but lived daily.

It follows from the insight that Christians were first called the Followers of the Way: the way of the Beloved Child of God to the Father, the way of the kingdom of peace with justice as it entered this world, the way of the light shining in communities that shared all things in common, giving to each according to their needs so that they prompted the observation, "See how those Christians love one another; there are no poor among them!" And finally it was the Way of the Cross, the way through the world and home to God, the Father, the Son, and the Spirit, for all in the community of Christians who sought to walk in the footsteps of Jesus the Lord.

In the Middle Ages towering cathedrals were built that became sites of pilgrimage, and many walked weeks or more to come into these places that resounded with dedication, holiness and the shared silence and belief of hundreds of thousands. For those who couldn't go on pilgrimage but could only make a visit, there were devotions that afforded the sense of what a pilgrimage to Jerusalem or Charters or Rome offered. On the floor of the cathedral of Chartres is the labyrinth. It winds around and around, eventually ending in the heart of the design. It represents a journey of body, mind, and soul, winding back to the source of life, to birth, and death. It is this same sort of concentrated walking of the Stations of the Cross that brings us back, as individuals and as a church, to our heart, our source, our beginnings and our ends: the cross of Christ. At their truest they are done in community, walking around the perimeter of the church or even in the neighborhood or the city itself, stopping along the way at sites representing the stations of each event in Jesus' journey from the garden to the cross on the hill outside the city, to the tomb in the garden so that those events can be remembered and reflected upon. There are moments for silence, for watching, for shared and ritual prayer; and then the community moves on to the next station. They are prime in the season of Lent and Holy Week, but also whenever the Church senses that there are peoples who are being drawn into their own way of suffering and having the burden of the Cross laid upon them by others today. And it seems in this new millennium that, sadly, every day somewhere in the world the broken and condemned Body of Christ is being led out to execution and forced to walk the Way of the Cross again.

The Stations of the Cross are a compass, a guide for the heart, a blueprint, and a source for sounding out our responses to what prevails and happens in our world today. They offer wise counsel on how to walk with dignity, with grace, with compassion, and with the freedom that the children of God have, no matter what we encounter along the way.

There is a story told in the Middle East of a man falsely accused and condemned to life in prison. He was bitter, angry, and despairing of the how to survive. One day a stranger came to visit, which was un-usual, but this prisoner was desperate for human company. It did not matter who it was. To his surprise the visitor brought him a prayer rug made by his wife. It seems the couple made these rugs and provided them for the prisoners who would be there for long periods of time as an aid to prayer, a comfort, a bit of beauty in the squalor of their bleak cells. He took it, thinking it would be good to sleep and sit on, afford-ing a bit of comfort. After a while he started using it daily, kneeling and bowing and praying on it, once, twice, up to five times a day. It became a necessity, something that sustained him and gave him hope. With time he looked at that rug and knew every detail and intricate line in the weaving and the pattern. And one day while he prayed, he saw the rug! He saw it for what it was—a design of a lock, a pattern of tunnels, a map that he could use to find his way to freedom. They say, he took it with him and walked out of his prison to live in freedom, forever grate-ful for the two strangers who gave him life again.

In a very real sense, that is what the Stations of the Cross do for us. They provide a pattern, a design of life that will save us, that will af-ford us a way to live with integrity and gracefulness in the midst of whatever situations of injustice, violence, deprivation, loss, or despair-ing situations we find ourselves, or the church finds itself in. We walk the Way of the Cross, all the way through the brutal destruction and dying of Jesus, and continue into the tomb where we will experience our baptism and begin to know the power of the resurrection in our own life—a dearer, truer life—here and now, that proclaims a fullness of life at the heart of the universe and our own bodies and souls.

The central prevailing symbol of the Stations is the person of Jesus and by extension the cross. The poet John Donne put it in a pecularily forthright manner, what it is we are to become in our devotion and practice of the Stations.

> *For when that Crosse ingrudg'd unto you stickes*
> *Then are you to your selfe a Crucifixe.*
>
> ("THE CROSSE")

There is no evading the pain of life, the sin of the world, the darkness that descends in every life, the injustices we all participate in, and, in the end, for all of us, the reality of death. But we move through these perils and toward this end with the fullness of life, with grace and the power of the Spirit and the company of the presence of God. Hidden in every station, suffused though the wood as blood saturates wood, is the sense of salvation, freedom, and the strength of God's love for us. This salvation cannot be forgotten. The way of the cross is the way of liberation, of victory, of justice, and the only human way to live in the midst of inhumaness and sin. This is a mystery, core to our faith. We call it the Paschal mystery, with all the images of the paschal lamb that is sacrificed, the command to mark the lintels of the doorposts and celebrate the passover of the angel of death and the passover of Jesus from the Last Supper, and Jesus' prayer in the garden, his burial, and his bursting forth from the tomb into another garden—as a new creation born in rejoicing and triumphing over death.

In the liturgy before the rite of Communion, we pray together, "O Lord, I am not worthy that you should come under my roof; only say the word and my soul shall be healed." This is spoken as the bread and wine—the Body and Blood of Christ—are lifted up. Say but the "word" . . . that word is the Cross. Our own bodies when we stand and stretch wide our arms and open our hearts are made in the sign of the cross. It is the sign of God approaching us to hold us all within the recesses of His own heart. This wood, this way, this word is our salvation and glory.

The Way of the Cross is also a way of protection and rescue. It is our hope and our faith, our lifestyle and proclamation of truth. It is the way of God's agony among us and how God draws our attention to injustice and sin among us. On the other hand, it is also how God draws near to us, painfully near in incarnation, in our neighbor and in the stranger's pain. And the Way is God's vindication of injustice. We walk it as witness to our hope in the midst of evil and despair, leaning on it as a sign of protection from the ultimate evil by telling the truth about life and death. This is where God stands in solidarity with all the innocent sufferers as a source of life for those threatened with death. Those sufferers announce and remind us that some evils cannot be rectified except by God and by final judgment and the mystery of death.

The days that commemorate these stations are all referred to as Good or as Holy, and so we walk them in holiness and grace and in goodness, attesting to the ultimate end of all life and creation. We walk in the midst of already being redeemed, reformed, remade into a new creation—transformed into the Body of Christ. These are the moments taken together that wrench us back from evil—evil that is personal, communal, and systematic—and hurl us mercifully into the arms of God, returning us again to freedom. We walk with the poor man Jesus, the Son of Justice, the one who judges the nations and the people with the power of justice because he has suffered unjustly at the hands of all men and women. These are moments and places of judgment, of wrenching, of chaos, of pain and death, and yet they are moments that defy the force and power of evil and steadfastly state that it does not last, it cannot hold. In these stations God grasps at us: a God bloodied and rejected and murdered. And this God continues to draw near to us in all of history, painfully close in all who suffer like him and with him, unjustly, needlessly, because of no escape from others' cruel intent or callousness and indifference. These are the moments that invite us to add our sufferings and those of our world to the sufferings of Christ and let us be washed in the blood of the Lamb.

And when we do the Stations we look into the mirror of God and get a glimpse of our dark hearts. Often we are not the victims of injustice. We do not often examine our lives in light of the Cross and see that we ourselves are evil-doers and perpetrators of evil. And we are asked if we follow in the footsteps of the suffering servant, obeying and following him, even unto death, death on a cross (Philippians 2:8). So many are caught in the horror of evil's consequences; we must not stand afar off so that their cry is muted and barely heard.

The devotion of doing the Stations affords us time to stand before the Cross, reverence it, and let it touch our skin and hearts again to make us human and to save us. First it is a time to see and remember God's pain as the pain of others. It is a time to confess to our guilt, our lack of action, how shallow and hesitant is our response to the sufferings of others, how half-heartedly we resist evil, never looking deeply into our own levels of collusion. We reflect and agonize over injustice and pray with Jesus to stand against and resist it and try to absorb what we can of it into our own flesh and lives and stop it there. It is a chance to examine whether our sufferings and pain come from closeness and compassion toward the suffering servant in the world today or from our own selfish determinations, or simply from being human.

These Stations and the reflections on our history and daily world occurences make it blatantly clear that we are as savage today as when Christ was crucified. And we are not allowed to distance ourselves from the consequences laid upon those who suffer because of our lack of action and care, or because we intend and do others harm. With Jesus we carry the cross, are stripped naked, betrayed, and rejected, condemned by those in authority and nailed to the sin and injustice in the world. They afford us time for confession, since we are all sinners, all caught in the illusions of grandeur, individuality, power, rights, privileges, racism, and nationalism, and enmeshed in all the philosophies that allow us to sustain our lifestyles, our ways that we have worked at so hard. But the Stations make us humble, empty us out, and realign us with the Body of Christ and recommit us to living nonviolence and bearing our share of the burden of the gospel. This is what unites us in communion with the blood of Christ and makes us the friends of God, his suffering servants who seek to fill up what is lacking in Christ's suffering and make the world whole again.

The Stations afford us endless entrances into home, where we are made more human and more in the image of God. They invite us to the folly and the wisdom of God, whose power is found in the sign of the Cross, and always freely offered to us. Along this Way we are drawn painfully close to each other, especially those who suffer, and in so doing we find ourselves close to God. These are moments and places where God looks at us with the merciless eyes of truth. And here is where God pleads with us in body and blood, hands, limbs, eyes, and guts to lament, console, to practice mercy, to have courage, to live without violence, to stand faithful, to have compassion, to mourn others' sorrows, to share one another's burdens, to be acquainted with infirmity and learn how not to break the bruised reed or put out the smoldering wick. (Isaiah 42:3). Here is the invitation of Jesus at the Last Supper to share the cup and drink the wine, to walk in blood, to walk in goodness, and fall into the arms of the Father, who will catch us, as he caught the body of Jesus; and then, with Christ, he will raise us up to new life, new freedom, and fresh creation that is ever becoming more human and holy. The arms of the Cross become the arms of God. It is good. So, let us go. Let us follow Jesus to the Cross and death and resurrection. Let us go with God.

Even in the fourteenth station, when Jesus lies dead in the tomb, we are summoned to see things as they are and not as they appear to be. We must remember that all these stations are as much about life as they are obviously about death. All is redeemed. All is grist for transformation and glory. Jesus will sleep in earth's arms. The ground knows it will never experience this kind of seeding again. Its heartbeats quicken and begin to hum, returned to the source of life even in dead flesh that refuses to decompose. All creation responds to the potency of genesis and life and will feed on the presence of this Body whose obedience has consequences for everything. Everything will stand up. The death grip will loosen. And the earth will begin mimicking a tight-fisted child kicking in the womb so that the mother jumps back startled by such energy, such assertion, such force of independent life within her. The earth will experience God stirring, and in the mysterious connection of all that is made, the sky, and waters, moon, and stars will all stretch, testing boundaries, begin to bud, soon to burst forth, opening the tomb, shoving aside stones that block and barricade, spring up and dawn. All creation will internally be shivering and shaking and dancing, for it will know new freedom after its long imprisonment. First earth, as it was in the beginning; then sky, waters, land shifts; then bird, beast, swimmer, crawlers; and then all the friends of God will breathe air that is the Spirit of God loose in the world again.

The Stations are powerful, even more so because they precede eastering, resurrection, glory, baptism, inspiriting, freeing, everything blooming, bursting, and dancing out of themselves because God raises this Crucified One from the dead, and we are all alive again. We are born to become divine again. We live in God and so we know joy. And we walk on, and on and on. Edith Stein, who walked into Christianity, into a Carmelite monastery, and finally into the gates of a concentration camp, wrote,

> O my God, fill my soul with holy joy, courage and strength to serve you. Enkindle your love in me and then walk with me along the next stretch of road before me. I do not see very far ahead, but when I have arrived where the horizon now closes down, a new prospect will open before me and I shall meet it in peace.

This, too, is the Way of the Cross, with stations and stopping points, places to linger and live along the way. We walk it alone, but all together. We walk it with God; and as believers, we trust it leads home. In fact, as Catherine of Siena wrote, startlingly, "For those who believe that Jesus Christ is Lord to the glory of the Father, in the embrace of

the Spirit, all the way home to heaven is home!" The Way of the Cross
is the Way, the Truth, and the Life, the presence and company of God
with us all the way home.

> It is better to allow our lives to speak for us than our words.
> God did not bear the cross only two thousand years ago. He
> bears it today, and he dies and is resurrected from day to day.
> It would be a poor comfort to the world if it had to depend on
> a historical God who died two thousand years ago. Do not,
> then, preach the God of history, but show him as he lives to-
> day through you.
>
> —MOHANDAS K. GANDHI

Suggestions for Praying the Stations of the Cross and Using This Book

1. Reflect upon the Stations alone, using these chapters as places
of beginning, as sources of meditation, or spiritual reading.

2. Use pieces of these longer meditations as part of the traditional
Stations of the Cross devotion in church. Select sections to read as reflections. Follow the ancient practice of beginning each station with
these words:

> We adore you, O Christ, and we praise you, because by your
> holy cross you have redeemed the world.

Then pause for quiet. Read the Scripture passage. Pause in silence.
Read a selected portion of the chapter for reflection. Pause again for
silent devotion and prayer. Then close that station with the prayer at
the end of the chapter, or one of your own choosing. Traditionally, as
there was movement from one station to the next, a psalm or a hymn

was sung, a verse for each station. (See notation at the end of this instruction for suggestions.)

3. During medieval times churches were often in almost total darkness, with only the light of fourteen candles lit at the Stations and others near the main altar. The atmosphere was stark, simple, sombre. The leader of the prayer, the priest, someone who carried the cross, and two servers with candles moved around the church, stopping at each station as the prayers and reflections were said, waiting on the silence as it built in the community. With the music, they would move to the next station, but not before taking the candle or taper burning in the niche or holder at that station and turning it over and snuffing it out on the floor with a loud thud, which would sound like a heartbeat (depending on what flooring there was). (Use cheesecloth or another material to protect your floor.) The sound is incredibly sad, mournful, and the church grows progressively darker as the Way of the Cross draws near to Jesus' death and burial, leaving the church in darkness at the end. After a period of silence, a prayer or a reading from the fifteenth station can be read, with a closing blessing sending the people forth to continue walking the Way of the Cross outside in the street and their lives.

4. In recent years many communities and parishes have walked the Stations of the Cross through their own city. They chose ahead of time fourteen stations, sites in the neighborhood where injustice, suffering, and evil were experienced. Prisons, places where people had been shot, where gangs and drugs proliferated, where there had been drunken driving accidents, drive-by shootings, drunken fights, places that stored or made weapons, immigration and welfare offices, empty lots—anyplace the community felt there had been and were currently situations and experiences of sin, evil, and injustice. A large cross was carried, with many people taking turns bearing the cross through the streets. Again, a similar pattern of prayer, reading, reflection, silence, and singing accompanied the cross as the people made their way through the Stations.

5. If a church has the more traditional stations, or no stations per se, the stations can be represented by symbols. Collection baskets for food for the poor, clothing items, green cards, identity papers, visiting passes, barbed wire, stones, collages of faces, newspaper clippings, crosses with names, broken dishes, pottery, candles, banners of color, shredded paper, broken glass—whatever captures the sense and content of that particular station. Always think in terms of less, rather than more, to make a statement with the symbol.

TRADITIONAL MUSIC SELECTIONS

Stabat Mater

Just a Closer Walk With Thee

O Sacred Head Surrounded

Were You There When They Crucified My Lord? (spiritual)

Before the Cross of Jesus (Ferdinand Blanchard)

OTHER MUSIC SELECTIONS

The Lord Hears the Cry of the Poor (Bob Dufford, North American Liturgy Resources)

Walking on This Journey (Monks of Weston Priory)

Via Crucis (Monks of Weston Priory)

Remember Your Love (Damiens, North American Liturgy Resources)

Remember Me, Stay With Me, and other selections (Taize)

Holy Darkness, Lover of Us All (Dan Schutte)

Celtic Laments

Russian Orthodox chants

Rachmaninoff: Vespers, op. 31

St. Matthew's Passion

Faure Requiem

Lamb of God, Kyrie, Lord Have Mercy

"You Lift Me High," ONCE IN A RED MOON, *Secret Garden album*

"Watch the Lamb" (Simeon of Cyrene), Ray Boltz

Barbar's Adagios for Strings

"The Silent Path," Robert Cox

First Station

■

JESUS PRAYS
IN THE GARDEN
OF OLIVES

■

SCRIPTURE: LUKE 22:39–42, 45–46

He went, as usual, to the Mount of Olives with the disciples following him. When they reached the place, he said to them, "Pray now, that you may be faithful to what God wants." Then he withdrew from them about a stone's throw, knelt down, and prayed, "O Holy One, if you are willing, remove this cup from me; yet, not my will but yours be done." . . . When he rose from prayer, he returned to his disciples but found them sleeping because of their grief. He said to them, "Why are you sleeping? Rise up and pray so that you may be faithful."

Or

SCRIPTURE: MARK 14:33–36

Jesus took Peter, James, and John with him to the garden. He was greatly distressed and troubled. He said to them, "My soul is sorrowful, even unto death. Remain here. Watch." He fell on the ground and prayed if it were possible, this hour might pass from him. "Abba, Father, all things are possible to you; remove this cup from me: yet not what I will, but what you will."

■　■　■　■　■　■

Prayers and love are learned in the hour when prayer has become impossible and your heart has turned to stone.

THOMAS MERTON

It begins: the Way of the Cross, the *Via Crucis*, as Jesus, the Holy One, turns his face toward Jerusalem and the destiny of all the prophets of God. This is the time of decision, of determination and conscious prayer in the face of the destruction that lies ahead. This is where Jesus begins to face down his fear. And it is where we, as his followers, begin to face down our fears. Death is close, but it is the death that is conceived in hate, in violence, leading to the deliberate, extinction of another's life. It is the death of the prophet, the truth-teller, the person who serves and obeys the will of God above the will of any nation, any government, any religious body, any group with affluence or power. His death will be a long time coming, in anguish, terrible aloneness, betrayal, and horror, the vicious horror that only human beings can inflict on one another.

Jesus enters the garden deliberately, in preparation, intending to face his fears by facing his God, his Father. His greatest fear is to offend his Father, to disobey his own calling, his integrity, and the word of God in his life. This is the prayer of hope and desperation, of acceptance and commitment, the cry for strength and endurance, the prayer that he might live, and if he must die, to die with hope, with steadfast belief in his Father, and if need be, without consolation. He prays to be faithful to what God wants, and exhorts his followers, already caught in the grip of grief and fear that grows palatable, to pray with him and to pray for themselves in this time of darkness.

The Father is the God of life, of love, of forgiveness and freedom for all. And he himself has come for life, life ever more abundant and creative. And so Jesus falls before his Father, on his knees, begging and pleading for life instead of the cup of bitterness that others will offer him as they wrest his life from him in violence. But this night, this garden will be the place of freedom and obedience for Jesus, and he will look and watch and pray. He will contemplate and will himself to a death of nonviolent and loving response toward all, even toward those who seek only to kill him, silence him, and stop such goodness and unbearable truth from existing in a human being in this world.

Contemplation is a long, loving look at reality, especially reality that is painful and hard to look at, but this is what Jesus does. He bends before his Father and his God and recommits himself in obedience to life, the life of the freedom of the children of God. He prays for peace, for holiness and wholeness even as his life begins to pour forth from him. He lives and faces terror and violent death and reveals to all how to exist in spite of the hate and harm that others intend for us. We must learn. We must imitate. We must pray and we must demonstrate again as we begin this journey to the cross that we are dedicated to a life of nonviolence and a life of contemplation, in obedience to our God, following on the way of our brother and master, Jesus.

Our history tells us of those who walked this way, struggling as Jesus did, seeking life in the face of death. Dietrich Bonhoeffer wrote in one of his journals while he was in prison, "Once Jesus bids you come and follow him, he bids you come and die." He sought to express his knowledge, born of prayer in the face of fear, this way:

> There is no way to peace along the way of safety. For peace
> must be dared. It is the great venture. It can never be safe.
> Peace is the opposite of security. To demand guarantees is to
> mistrust, and this mistrust in turn brings forth war. Peace
> means to give oneself altogether to the law of God, wanting no
> security, but in faith and obedience laying the destiny of the
> nations in the hand of Almighty God, not trying to direct it for
> selfish purposes. Battles are won, not with weapons, but with
> God. They are won where the way leads to the cross.
>
> (DIETRICH BONHOEFFER, NO RUSTY SWORDS: LETTERS,
> LECTURES AND NOTES, 1928–1936 [COLLINS, 1965])

Some people do this with their whole life, as a way of living, of resisting evil, and others find themselves having to face their fears and resist because of history, because of how the world of evil and violence intrudes upon them rudely and unexpectedly. In the 1970s in Argentina the military dictatorship brutally "disappeared" anyone who spoke out against injustice, against the regime, against the military, or anyone the dictatorship suspected of support for the opposition, sometimes two or three or more members of the same family. Husbands and wives, pregnant women, single men and women, leaders and organizers—all suffered the same fate: being "disappeared." It was their mothers, many of them elderly, but from all age groups, who responded to the horror by gathering together publically in the Plaza de Mayo in the downtown area They gathered, congregated as they would in church, carrying placards like banners, chanting, praying, mourning, crying out their frustrations with the military and the government bureaucracies, all of which refused them a hearing or any information on their loved ones. They came, week after week, day after day, facing the prospect that they too would be recognized and later suffer the same fate as their children and loved ones. Their stories are told, still, now thirty years or more later. Listen. Watch. Pray.

When the women congregated at the plaza, police snapped at them to keep moving. So the fourteen mothers walked the plaza in slow circles. They kept coming back to protest, braving nightsticks, police dogs, and military spies who infiltrated the group and killed three leaders.

"They say the Mothers of the Plaza de Mayo were fearless," said Maria Adela Antokolez, now eighty-five, who moves with slow, tottering steps and enormous dignity, "but we were scared to death. We learned to walk with fear, to live with fear. We had an obligation to find our children."

The mothers still march every Thursday afternoon demanding justice. The ritual moves bystanders to tears and applause. The women are elderly and fragile now. They walk arm in arm, hunched beneath the white head scarves that have become an international symbol of the fight for human rights.

"We never found our children," Maria Adela said. "But in

the plaza we went to school. We told our story fifty times. We
cried together. It was our educational academy. The plaza
saved us from the madhouse." . . . It spread by word of mouth.
When Cortázar, our great writer, heard about it in Paris, he
said, "The mothers are out, the military have already lost."

(JACK KORNFIELD, *AFTER THE ECSTASY, THE LAUNDRY* [NEW YORK:

BANTAM DOUBLEDAY DELL, 2001], p. 232)

Others discover and seek out this stance of contemplation and
nonviolent love and living through the Scriptures, through association
with prophets and monks, or through the grace of God in prayer.
Dorothy Day, in the company of Thomas Merton, Daniel Berrigan, and
many others, spoke for many when she wrote,

We were setting our faces against the world, against things as
they are, the terrible injustice of our capitalist industrial system, which lives by war and by preparing for war; setting our
faces against race hatreds and all the nationalistic strivings.
But especially we wanted to act against war and the preparation for war; nerve gas, guided missiles, the testing and stock-
piling of nuclear bombs, conscription, the collection of income
tax—against the entire military state. We made our gesture; we
disobeyed a law. . . .

(*CATHOLIC WORKER*, 1957, AFTER A JAIL STAY)

Our heritage is filled with prayers that echo Jesus' own words to his
beloved Father as he prayed in the garden. Charles de Foucauld
prayed: "Father, I abandon myself into Your hands; do with me what
You will. Whatever You may do, I thank you: I am ready for all, I accept
all. Let only Your will be done in me and in all Your creatures—I wish
no more than this, Lord." Even more simply and to the point for many
of us, Peter Julian Eymard prays, "Lord, I dare not say I love Thee, but
I WILL love thee."

Obedience to the will of God is the only way to face down our fears in a world intent on killing, on silencing the truth and keeping to its own way. We walk with Jesus into the garden, praying with him, choosing instead to walk his way, the Way of the Cross, to walk in life, in nonviolent love and contemplation. Let us go with Jesus to God. Amen.

Let us pray: Lord, always you went to your Father, seeking his will and obeying his word to you. This was an integral part of your daily life, and you knew this night was coming long before others did because you prayed and because you saw what was going on around you in others' lives and in the world that sought to silence your word of truth and compassion. May we watch with you. May we pray with you. May we share your burden of knowing what human beings are capable of doing to one another in hate and yet fearing only God, not what others can do to us. May we fall with you before the Father and begin this Way of the Cross, saying with you, Father, if this cup can pass me by, let it be. But if I must drink it because of others' choices, then may I drink it with all those who seek to live for love and bring your kingdom more truly into our world. Amen.

Second Station

■

JESUS
IS BETRAYED
BY JUDAS

■

SCRIPTURE: MATTHEW 26:45–49

*Then Jesus once again came back from his prayer to the disciples
and said to them, "Sleep and rest now because as you can plainly
see, everything is culminating here and I will be handed over to
sinners. Rise, then, and let us go. See, my betrayer is at hand."
While he was still speaking, Judas arrived. He was one of the
Twelve, and he had with him a large crowd sent from the chief
priests and the elders of the people and they carried swords and
clubs. Now the betrayer had given them a sign: "The one I will
kiss," he had told them, "is the man: seize him." Upon arriving,
Judas immediately came up to Jesus and said, "Greetings, Rabbi!"
and kissed him.*

Or

SCRIPTURE: MARK 14:43, 45–46

*And immediately while he was still speaking, Judas came, one of
the Twelve, and with him a crowd with swords and clubs, from
the chief priests and the scribes and elders. . . . And when he
came, he went up to him at once, and said, "Master!" And he
kissed him. And they laid hands on him and seized him.*

■ ■ ■ ■ ■ ■

*God does not require of us the martydom of the body; he requires
only the martyrdom of the heart and the will.*

JOHN VIANNEY

The first steps and the first confrontation are perhaps the hardest, the most terrible to bear. Was the betrayal expected? Did Jesus know his disciples and friends well? Does he know us well and see into our hearts and faltering faith? Judas is described as one of the Twelve, one of the inner circle, the ones to whom he entrusted his message of forgiveness and love, of good news to the poor, of healing, and hope for the kingdom of God to reign upon the earth even now. There was a closeness, an intimacy, a shared tenderness among them all. They ate together, prayed together and walked the roads of Galilee together. They went up to Jerusalem and to the Passover feasts together, singing and waiting for the coming of God's presence and justice among them and their nation so long in bondage.

This is the pain of the heart, of the mind and soul. Susan Sontag once said that there are times when "the problem is how not to avert one's glance. How not to give way to the impulse to stop looking . . . this insistence on staring down—on reading—the unbearable, the too intimate . . . of refractions, revelations . . . complex interplay and correspondence . . . sights crossed by sounds, of visionary transformations" (in the introduction to Edward Hirsch's *Transforming Vision: Writers on Art*, Art Institute of Chicago [Boston: Little, Brown and Co., 1994]. She was speaking in reference to her looking at Francisco Goya's painting, "The Disaster of War," and lamenting that such a reality existed. But she could just as truly be describing the disaster of betrayal. Sometimes living with memory, with the thought of what friends, those who shared your soul and dreams, will do to you is worse than taking a bullet or having someone stab your flesh. There is a way of bleeding from one's soul.

The journey begins, still in the garden, among friends and now a crowd, a mob armed with clubs and swords, is brought in from outside. This is a form of personal violence, and there is no consolation here. This will mar the face of Jesus—where Judas kisses him—and his heart, where the words mock him: "Master" . . . "Rabbi" . . . It is executed in public in the presence of the other disciples and preplanned with his enemies and strangers intent on being in on the taking, the laying hands on him and seizing his life.

This is evil that is insidious, disheartening; it seeps into Jesus' own broken and troubled soul, but it comes from and affects the other eleven of his company. It begins the damage to the community that follows Jesus because it is so internal, so divisive. Yeats, the poet, wrote, "Almost always truth and lies are mixed together." He could have been describing any group, Jesus' own band of followers, and today, his church, which must deal with internal discord, bitter betrayals, and personal failures that debilitate and unravel the very core of a community. And yet, this was not what Jesus intended. He told his disciples, all of us, that we were not his servants, but his friends! This very same night he declared openly to all who would take it to heart, "You are my friends if you do what I command you. I do not call you servants any longer, because the servant does not know what the master is doing; but I have called you friends, because I have made known to you everything that I have heard from my Father. You did not choose me, but I chose you" (John 15:14–16). And Judas decides not to accept that gracious offering of friendship and turns upon his teacher, his master and friend. Somehow within the shared confines of one's own, the refusal and the rejection take on cosmic proportions and heightened significance that is almost unbearable. Judas has chosen.

The alternative? There is one, of course. J. R. Tolkien, in *The Lord of the Rings*, tells the story of another group, a band of Hobbits, of friends, and when the forces of evil pursue them to the edge of death these ordinary characters do not forsake one another but choose instead to sacrifice, to stand by one another and to hold out together against the evil that threatens all the earth. Frodo, who bears the burden of the ring, turns to his simple companion and friend, Sam, and whispers to him, "I am glad that you are here with me, here at the end of things, Sam." It is enough. It is enough to brave anything, not so much for any cause, but for another, for a friend.

But Judas denies Jesus that presence, that honoring and that love.

And the denial is worse for the kiss, the use of a symbol of such regard, of such trust and human power. C. S. Lewis wrote, "Everyone says forgiveness is a lovely idea, until they have something to forgive." And now Jesus has so much to forgive his friend, Judas Iscariot, one of the Twelve, remembered forever now as the traitor. This second station stares us straight in the face and forcibly asserts that we, too, are such traitors. We betray our first intensity of love with God in our baptisms. We betray our promise to "live in the freedom of the children of God." We betray each other's trust with lies, with slander and divisions and personal agendas and abuse of power, by forcing others to do what we want them to do. And we betray God's trust in us, as the friends of God, by our own sin that tears at the community of the Church and mocks the gospel in the wider world.

Judas's kiss is the signal for the arrest of Jesus. It sets in motion the process that will stop the kingdom coming into the world, will stop Jesus' voice and life. He uses his privileged relationship with Jesus to enable the religious and political system to destroy life. This station reminds us that whenever we use our religion, as individuals, or as groups within the church, to act in tandem with political and economic groups that arrest the voice of truth or destroy others, then we are Judas. Judas has been made responsible for what happened to Jesus, and we are to be held accountable for our arresting of goodness with a kiss of betrayal. But Jesus' essence could be summed up in one line: "Father, forgive them, for they know not what they are doing" (Luke 23:34). No matter what, this is Jesus' legacy, Jesus' blessing and gift to all of us who are now the friends of God because of our relationship with Jesus, his beloved.

But what of Judas the traitor, the sinner, who is not so different than the rest of us really? So often we are told that Judas is condemned forever to hell and it is left at that. But there is a tradition, not often told, a legend, that says otherwise. It is said that when Judas died, committing suicide in despair, not even hell would take his soul in. Instead he was sentenced to the far reaches of the north, in ice and snow, his soul trapped in the body of a wild creature, where he would spend forever howling his sin and being lost in the frozen reaches, alone, despised, and hated by all decent human beings. And that is where he is even now. But the story goes on to say something wondrous, startling, and full of risk. It is foretold that one night Judas, as he is lost and forsaken by all, will come upon a human dwelling place filled with light and laughter, music, and the company of friends. It will be a bitter sight for him, so long without companionship, exiled from all human relationships, and he will howl even more pitifully. And then the door will open wide, the light spilling out into the dark and snow, and a lone man will stand silouettted in the bright blinding light. And Judas will hear his name called out: softly, with tenderness that is unbearable, surely as once he was known, almost familiar from far away and long ago. He will be drawn inevitably to that voice, the sound of the Word of God, his Master and friend, Jesus. And Judas will draw near, crawling closer as he is called again and again by name. Finally he will lie at the feet of Jesus, and in the still of night he will hear words so unbelievable, so freeing, that his soul will break and shatter like ice. The master will say, "The night is filled with light and the room is filled with friends. The bread is broken and shared around. The wine is drawn and the company awaits the toast, but I have waited long for you, before I pour the wine. Welcome home, Judas, my friend." And the one so long lost will come in again.

Is it just a story? Or is it the good news of God? We are all forgiven, always, for everything. God's drawing near to us in Jesus' and his lingering love in the Spirit bring us back home times without end. We are bound together in the mysterious freedom of the children of God. And God's power in Jesus will never die. Our God will never betray us. The master waits with the door open and the invitation extended, whispered, and shouted again and again, forever.

John of the Cross, an old friend of God, once wrote to his friends in the company of Carmel, "Live in faith and hope, though it be in darkness, for in the darkness God protects the soul. Cast your care upon God for you are His and He will not forget you. Do not think that He is leaving you alone, for that would be to wrong him." We are his, and he does not forget us—not ever. Jesus is handed over to sinners. Jesus is handed over to us. It is our responsibility, our grace, and our terrible choice: to kiss Jesus and arrest the goodness of God or to be converted so that God will call us friends.

Let us pray: Jesus, you call us friends and you share with us all you know of the Father and the deepest dreams and hopes of your soul. May we honor that trust you put in us and be faithful to you as friends. May we never betray your love for us, but if we do, help us to remember that your forgiveness and love is always stronger than our lack of love and sin. You kiss us always with your love. Since we cannot really kiss you back in this world, may we turn toward others and welcome them, kissing them with the kindness of forgiveness and reconciliation. Amen.

Third Station

■

**JESUS IS CONDEMNED
TO DEATH
BY THE SANHEDRIN**

■

SCRIPTURE: MARK 14:55–56, 60–65

The chief priests with the whole Sanhedrin were busy soliciting testimony against Jesus that would lead to his death, but they could not find any. Many people gave false evidence against Jesus, but their stories did not agree. . . . The high priest rose to his feet before the court and began to interrogate Jesus: Have you no answer to what these men testify against you?" But Jesus remained silent; he made no reply. Once again the high priest interrogated him: "Are you the Messiah, the Son of the Blessed One?" Then Jesus answered: "I am; and you will see the Son of Man seated at the right hand of the Power and coming with the clouds of heaven." At that the high priest tore his robes and said: "What further need do we have of witnesses? You have heard the blasphemy. What is your verdict?" They all concurred in the verdict "guilty," with its sentence of death. Some of them then began to spit on him. They blindfolded him and hit him, saying, "Play the prophet!" while the officers manhandled him.

■ ■ ■ ■ ■ ■

We who lived in concentration camps can remember the men who walked through the huts comforting others, giving away their last piece of bread. They may have been few in number, but they offer sufficient proof that everything can be taken away from a man but one thing: the last of the human freedoms—to choose one's attitude in any given set of circumstances, to choose one's own way."

VIKTOR FRANKL, MAN'S SEARCH FOR MEANING

Jesus' presence on earth, his preaching of good news to the poor, his company with the outcast, his eating with those who did not live up to the expectations of the religious laws—all this leads Jesus inevitably to this tribunal, this hastily convened religious court. But it has already been decreed by the authorities, who live in a contrived collusion with the Romans occupying their country, that this man is dangerous and should die. Jesus is a source of hope for the majority of the people, who live as slaves in occupied territory, who toil for an invader, who are beaten down by history and are taxed by their own people's greed as ruthlessly as they are humiliated by the Roman forces. Jesus' preaching has seeded small shoots of an alternative future for the poor.

Jesus did not so much identify with "the wretched of the earth" as he befriended them! He sought out the company of the beggars, the lepers, and the sick, the public sinners and slackers, the tax collectors, and the unclean ritually and socially. He ate with them! He told them his stories and they found themselves wanting to live those images of his Father's kingdom of shared food, forgiveness, and a family based on obedience to the will of God, who truly was the God of life and justice! Jesus from the moment he first appears in Galilee is a sign of contradiction, formenting revolution through telling the truth about the state of the world, the reality of evil, and the eye of God, who judges in a different vein altogether than courts of law, whether they be religious canons, ecclesiastical courts, or government legal systems. In a word, this Jesus provoked a crisis of faith, a critical mass that demanded a choice by everyone who claimed to believe in righteousness and was waiting for God's will to be done in the world.

Jesus quickly became a scandal to theologians, scribes, priests, and lawyers. He couldn't bear the lies, the injustice, the laying of heavy burdens on widows and the poor while those who offered sacrifices and planned the liturgies lived on the money stolen from others who gave out of their pittance and their very sustenance for survival. In story and in sermon, Jesus laid bare the outrages of those who claimed to believe in God but cared not for the children of God. Now he stands before

the Sanhedrin, falsely accused because this court can't bear to even re-
peat the truth of his stinging words that have ground like salt into the
wounds that he has opened up with his preaching.

The writer William Faulkner encourages his readers to practice this
kind of refusal to participate in the inequities and injustices of the
world:

> Some things you must always be unable to bear. Some things
> you must never stop refusing to bear. Injustice and outrage,
> dishonor and shame. No matter how young you are and how
> old you have got. Not for kudos and not for cash. Your picture
> in the paper nor money in the bank. Just refuse to bear them.

They seek false witnesses against him, bribing them, trying to set
him up for the kill—literally. And Jesus has steadfastly pursued the
path of witnessing to the honor of God, the care of the poor, and the
coming of justice, as every prophet before him. It is burden enough
that there is such evil rampant in the world, but it is even more unbearable that it is couched in religious language, enforced by liturgy
that validates and confirms the dominant systems of the world as they
economically and politically deprive the world of dignity and hope. Ca-
pitulation to organized and systematic evil, as part of a bargain struck
for a deal that allows for a bit of leeway, a half-hearted devotion to God,
and a pragmatic acceptance of evil, enrages Jesus. He practiced a
liturgy that symbolically overthrew the collusion between the money-
changers in the temple and the sellers of the sacrifical victims that
gouged the poor and gave lip-service to worshipping God while making
a profit on the Roman currency.

Jesus is dangerous to society, to the status quo, and to contemporary piety. This clarity of preaching cannot be allowed to continue. It is
like a cold, a virus that infects all those who suffer and who live under
conditions that only worsen, in a world that blames those who are poor
and who do not live up to religious expectations. Dorothee Solle pin-

points why Jesus instilled such fear into the minds and hearts of those
in authority. "We are afraid of religion because it interprets rather than
just observes. Religion does not confirm that there are hungry people in
the world; it interprets the hungry to be our brethren whom we allow to
starve." This is true religion, and Jesus is as truthful as anyone can
bear. And so he must be condemned to death. It matters not that he is
innocent.

Jesus stands condemned. He stands with everyone who has stood
before tribunals and courts, without lawyer or counsel, not understand-
ing the language of the culture, those who run out of time in their ap-
peals, those who are tried as adults though they are juveniles, children
or mentally retarded or uneducated. He stands with those falsely accused, those whose face imprisonment and death because evidence is
not allowed to be entered into their trial proceedings, and those who
are caught in a system that has decided this was the time to make a
statement on being tough on crime—"three strikes and you're out"—or
appeal to a constitutency that is mired in its own fears and insecurity
and so feels the need to single out someone for punishment. He stands
with those who disappeared into and were lost in the beauracracies and
overcrowding, or were just in the wrong place at the wrong time. Often
these are the fringe folk of the world: indigenous, immigrant farmwork-
ers and peasants, labor and community organizers, student leaders, del-
egates of the Word, advocates for those without a voice, the landless,
and those who have lost their civil rights and their livelihoods to corporations and governments.

Yet when Jesus is accused, he does not defend himself! He stands
silent. His defense is his life, his words. Only when he is asked who he
is does he respond. "Are you the Messiah, the Son of the Blessed
One?" Yes! He has called God his beloved Father and taught his disciples to call upon God as "our Father." But Jesus is intent to be clear,
and so he uses the ancient prophetic language of the coming of judgment and justice upon the world. He turns the tables on the assembly,
daring to claim intimacy with the power of the One who will judge the

world and all its inhabitants with justice. He is judging them even as he stands before them. He has only ever spoken the truth, and the authorities can rely on that! Jesus' words are carefully chosen and strongly stated: "*I AM*," and those words are used to kindle a self-righteous rage that will draw those who have been summoned to be a part of the proceedings to unanimously declare that Jesus "deserves death."

Those words "deserves death" are vile, ominous, evil. Does anyone deserve death? Do not all deserve life, life ever more abundant? It is a line that has been used in other settings to either validate the execution and killing of other human beings or to call to account those who think they can usurp the judgment of God. *The Lord of the Rings* uses those exact words when Frodo remembers a conversation he had once with the wise Gandalf about killing Gollum, who has brought such destruction and chaos into the world. Once Bilbo had had the chance to kill him, and Frodo had cried out

> "What a pity that he did not stab the vile creature, when he had a chance!"
> "Pity? It was pity that stayed his hand. Pity, and Mercy: Not to strike without need."
> "I do not feel any pity for Gollum. He deserves death."
> "Deserves death! I daresay he does. Many that live deserve death. And some die that deserve life. Can you give that to them? Then be not too eager to deal out death in the name of justice. . . . Even the wise cannot see all ends."

Certainly we abhor it when the innocent die or are cold-bloodedly condemned to death, but why do we not find it equally abhorrent that we could kill anyone in the certainty that they "deserve death"? Do we lie to ourselves and claim for ourselves what belongs by right to God alone—decisions on the life and death of all his creatures, his children? Do we seek to validate our own sin of murder, of condemning anyone to death for whatever reason and still lay claim to being believers in the

God that Jesus the Christ, the Holy One, serves, even unto death, a wrongful death at the hands of religious people? Is the silent witness against us Jesus and anyone we have judged harshly? Do we stand convicted?

Jesus stands before the Sanhedrin. Jesus stands before us, his presence judging us. Do we spit on God? Do we go after the prophets in our midst? Do we know who tells us the truth yet manhandle them? Do we blindfold those who see us too clearly and mock those who reveal us as standing in opposition to the Christ, the Son of the Blessed One? We stop at this station and stand before the Suffering Servant, the Lamb of God. Will he speak to us?

Let us pray: Lord, you stand already convicted before the trial in the Sanhedrin. False witnesses are brought against you, but the verdict has been decided before you were arrested. Lord, so many in our society know this experience. Not just those accused and tried unjustly and condemned but those caught in a system that unfairly targets the poor, the immigrant, and those who are without access to the structures of society. You stand in the presence first of your Father, as you stand before those who disrespect you and will arrange to have you killed. May you always find us standing with those who need your presence and the company of those who seek justice and truth for all. Amen.

Fourth Station

■

JESUS
IS DENIED
BY PETER

■

SCRIPTURE: LUKE 22:54–62

They led him away under arrest and brought him to the house of the high priest while Peter followed at a distance. Later they lighted a fire in the middle of the courtyard and were sitting beside it, and Peter sat among them. A servant girl saw him sitting in the light of the fire. She gazed at him intently, then said, "This man was with Jesus." But Peter denied it, saying, "Woman, I do not know him." A little later someone else saw him and said, "You are one of them, too?" But Peter said, "No sir, not I!" About an hour after that another spoke more insistently: "This man was certainly with him; for he is a Galilean." Peter responded, "My friend, I do not know what you are talking about." At the very moment he was saying this, a cock crowed. The Lord turned around and looked at Peter, and Peter remembered the word that the Lord had spoken to him: "Before the cock crows today, you will deny me three times." He went out and wept bitterly.

Or

SCRIPTURE: MARK 14: 66–72

While Peter was down in the courtyard, one of the servant girls of the high priest came along. When she noticed Peter warming himself, she looked at him more closely and said, "You, too, were with Jesus of Nazareth." But he denied it: "I do not know what you are talking about! What are you getting at?" Then he went out into the gateway [at that moment a cock crowed]. The servant girl, keeping an eye on him, started again to tell the bystanders, "This man is one of them." Once again he denied it. A little later the bystanders said to Peter once more, "You are certainly one of them! You are a Galilean, are you not?" He began to curse, and to swear. "I do not even know the man you are talking about!" Just then a second cockcrow was heard, and Peter recalled the prediction Jesus had made to him: "Before the cock crows twice you will deny me three times." He broke down and began to cry.

■ ■ ■ ■ ■ ■

Let there be such oneness between us that when one cries, the other tastes salt.

ROSABELLE BELIEVE

Jesus is in the midst of his enemies. His execution has been set in motion, and Peter follows, though at a distance, careful and trying to dis-
appear into the shadows. But it grows cold in the night, and Peter
approaches the fire and is caught in its light, and recognized. This is
Peter's test, his chance to give witness, to speak truthfully and stand
with his teacher, his Rabbi, his Master and his friend. Jesus had told
him and all the disciples earlier that night to pray that they would not
be put to the test, to watch and pray with him, lest they fail. But Peter
is afraid that he will be drawn into the net of hate and intrigue that has
been set in motion. Peter is ashamed of being associated with Jesus.
And when he is associated with Jesus he reacts with anger, wanting to
distance himself more and more from any relationship with the one
who is condemned and now outcast from his own band of followers,
his own people and religion and soon, from the crowd and the whole
people of his nation.

He is questioned now by a servant girl who really has little power,
though she is in the employ of the high priest. She is persistent. She's
seen him with Jesus. Then others collectively scrutinize him and pick
up on his demeanor and accent that betray him as a Galilean. Three
times he backs off and does not want to be thought of being related to
Jesus. He begins with a simple denial. He progresses to being indignant. And at the end, he is vehement, cursing and swearing, disowning
any knowledge of Jesus. He even refers to a stranger as "friend," not
wanting to be seen as friend to Jesus, who is undergoing a trial by liars
and false accusers inside the house.

This is why Peter was born into the world. This is why Peter was
called and chosen as one of the Twelve. This is why Peter was singled
out to be in the inner circle of the three along with James and John,
privileged to pray with Jesus, to see a glimpse of his essence on the
mountain of the Transfiguration, and to be included in his trust and
shared authority and power as leader in his absence. But when faced
with the prospect of pain, with the possibility of suffering because of
his closeness to Jesus, with the risk of being truthful and being a friend

to the one who has called him by a new name and drawn him into the family of his Father, Peter doesn't just balk, he resists and decries the very goodness of Jesus. He betrays his teacher utterly.

He starts small, feigning ignorance of who Jesus is, asking, "What are you getting at?" He's intent on his own safety. Then he gets better at lying. He flat out denies the connection. And then he reacts with venom and utterly severs any relationship with Jesus at all. Did this denial come out of nowhere? No, it is part of a pattern that started when he heard Jesus' preaching about the Cross, and it continued whenever Jesus spoke of pain, of what it could be mean to be a disciple. Jesus first announces and begins to teach the Cross, that he would suffer much and be rejected and put to death, and Peter's response is quick and strong. He remonstrates with Jesus and is told in a reprimand, "Get out of my sight, you satan! You are not judging by God's standards but by man's" (Mk. 8:32–33). Peter heard Jesus' words: "He summoned the crowd with his disciples and said to them: 'If you wish to come after me, you must deny your very self, take up your cross, and follow in my steps'" (Mk. 8:34). This part of the Jesus' teachings Peter rejects, piece by piece, so that when the hard times come, it is not surprising that he fails.

And us: when do we begin as Peter did, feigning ignorance about someone, an incident, an issue or a teaching of the gospel? Or we deny, either point blank or by obvious silence, that we are connected to Christ, being baptized and calling ourselves followers of the Suffering Servant? When do we or the groups we are a part of in the church refuse to stand in solidarity with others or ignore and resist the teachings of Christ because they may put us in a poor light with others, or in jeopardy? Do we have the same difficulty as Peter in even beginning "to deny our very selves"? This concept is not one that most of us dwell upon often or practice frequently. Traditionally the first steps of denying oneself began with the practices of prayer, penance, fasting, and almsgiving as ways of proclaiming that we were being reconciled to God, atoning for our sin and collusion with evil, and attempting to balance the forces of evil and goodness in the world.

The concept of sacrifice, of giving over utterly something to God, is another form of denying ourselves. The core of this discipline is obedience to the needs of the community, knowing the will of God for us through the care of the poor, the corporal works of mercy and justice for others. And most clearly, this denial of self has been revealed in moral decision making, personally and as members of the Church. This station makes us stop and question who it is that we disassociate ourselves from in order to protect our own skins. Do we feign ignorance on issues of ethics: the death penalty, abortion, human rights and civil rights, and the protection of immigrants and those on welfare and in need of the basic necessities of life? Do we go further in our denial and attack those who speak out for justice and confront the hard issues economically, politically, and nationally?

Peter's denial was not just a personal weakness. He was in a leadership position, honored as the one who spoke for the group, and was second in command (when Jesus wasn't around). But his choice to publicly deny his place in the community at the side of Jesus had massive repercussions for the other disciples. They ran and hid, and from this point on in the Way of the Cross there is no mention of the disciples again in the Passion narrative. The sheep are scattered, routed, and demoralized. Peter's sin tore open the seams that held them together.

It didn't have to be this way. Jesus is led out of the High Priest's house, condemned to death. They have started to attack him physically, manhandling him, mocking him and spitting at him. He looks up and catches sight of Peter. One glance and it is all painfully clear. With each step, he walks more alone as evil overwhelms his friends and disciples. What kind of glance would have passed between them if Jesus had overheard a word of courage, of loyalty, of faithfulness? But Peter was out of practice.

There is an old story from an Associated Press clipping that strikes us to our heart's core and reveals how to stand with those facing pain and the threat of death.

Mark Lowry, 13, is a seventh grader at Cross Lutheran School, in Yorkville, Illinois. He has leukemia. By the end of the week when the school's 15 other seventh and eighth grade boys discovered that Mark would undergo chemotherapy and lose his hair, only two of the 16 weren't bald. One was waiting for the weekend for his clipping. The other was Mark, who came home from his treatment with a full head of hair.

How long do the boys plan to go hairless as a show of solidarity with their classmate? "Until Mark grows his hair back" was the unanimous response.

But it takes practice to stand with others facing pain or death, and it helps if you don't have to do it all alone. We should practice on the small stuff so that we will be better able to stand together for what we believe and for those we love, who may someday need our support. And it will always come. How to be a friend to God in Jesus? How to be a friend to those condemned unjustly, those caught in the hate of others' crossfire? How to be a friend to those who look to us to stand up for our faith and encourage the weak who falter? Pray with me. Watch with me. Begin by denying your very self.

Let us pray: Deliver us, O Lord, from cowardice and an easy familiarity with you that assumes you think like us and have our agendas in mind. Remind us again and again to pray and seek to judge by your standards and listen to the hard words of facing pain and suffering together with you. May we practice on all those who share our lives, our workplaces, our schools, and political situations, and then reach out to those who are bound to you in the bonds of shared advocacy and justice on behalf of the poor and the outcast of the earth, who are your presence among us. May we learn to treat them with as much tender regard as we would treat you, and to stand up for them with all our strength and courage, knowing it is you we call our friend. Amen.

The Fifth Station

■

JESUS
IS JUDGED
BY PILATE

■

SCRIPTURE: LUKE 23:20–25

*Pilate addressed them again, for he wanted Jesus to be the one he
released. But they only shouted back, "Crucify him. Crucify him!"
He said the them for the third time, "What wrong is this man
guilty of? I have not discovered anything about him that calls for
the death penalty. I will therefore chastise him and release him."
But they demanded with loud cries that he be crucified, and their
shouts increased in violence. Pilate then decreed that what they
demanded should be done. He released the one they asked for,
who had been thrown into prison for insurrection and murder,
and delivered Jesus up to their wishes.*

Or

SCRIPTURE: MARK 15:1–15

*As soon as it was daybreak the chief priests, with the elders and
scribes (that is, the whole Sanhedrin) reached a decision. They
bound Jesus, led him away, and handed him over to Pilate. Pilate
interrogated him: "Are you the King of the Jews?" "You are the one
who is saying it," Jesus replied. The chief priests, meanwhile,
brought many accusations against him. Pilate interrogated him
again: "Surely you have some answer? See how many accusations
they are leveling against you. But greatly to Pilate's surprise, Jesus
made no further response.*

Now on the occasion of a festival he would release for them one prisoner—any man they asked for. There was a prisoner named Barabbas jailed along with the rebels who had committed murder in the uprising. When the crowd came up to press their demand that he honor the custom, Pilate rejoined, "Do you want me to release the King of the Jews for you?" He was aware, of course, that it was out of jealousy that the chief priests had handed him over. Meanwhile, the chief priests incited the crowd to have him release Barabbas instead. Pilate again asked them, "What am I to do with the man you call the King of the Jews?" They shouted back. "Crucify him!" Pilate protested, "Why? What crime has he committed?" They only shouted the louder, "Crucify him!" So Pilate, who wished to satisfy the crowd, released Barabbas to them: and after he had had Jesus scourged, he handed him over to be crucified.

■ ■ ■ ■ ■ ■

*Violence does not necessarily take people by the throat
and strangle them.
Usually it demands no more than an oath of allegiance
from its subjects.
They are required merely to become accomplices in its lies.*
ALEKSANDR SOLZHENITSYN

This station is hinged to the judgment of the Sanhedrin. They could, as the religious tribunal, condemn a person to death and hand down a verdict of "guilty and deserving of death," but as a nation under the heel of Rome, they could not actually put a person to death. So it was time to change tactics. They as religious leaders and teachers find Jesus dangerous. Now they must convince Pilate, the Roman governor, that Jesus is also dangerous to him in the arena of politics, nationalism, the empire, and its agenda. So they begin by changing the language they use about Jesus. They could convince those in their own circle that he deserved to die by asserting that he had claimed that his relationship with God was one of intimacy, of beloved son, of shared power, prophet and judge, but for Pilate, he is called the King of the Jews. Just the thought of someone claiming to be a king in occupied territory could foment a revolution that could be costly in time, military deployment, and general disruption of Rome's plan for using the country's resources and people.

But, strangely, it is Pilate who balks at their intentions. He interrogates Jesus again and again, and silence is Jesus' firm response in the face of the lies and accusations. His demeanor and the way he presents himself before Pilate impresses him. Somehow Jesus has affected him, and he wants to release him. He finds no cause for the death penalty, or any penalty for that matter, and he is shrewd enough to know that the real reason Jesus stands before him is the jealousy of the leaders of the people. But he is a weak man and will not stand against them. Though he protests their request, he will not stop the killing of an innocent man. His duty is to do what will most benefit the state.

He is at his core a politican, and he obeys his superiors, careful to secure his own position of power and control of the people. He searches for some shred of legality to proclaim a death sentence and is trapped by the crowd into honoring the custom of releasing anyone they want, though it is certainly not the one he would like to give them. Barabbas, who was part of an insurrection against the Roman military and is a murderer, is a much more immediate danger and threat to

Rome than this man who stands before him. But the leaders have incited the people, stirred the crowd into a mob that quickly becomes bloodthirsty, retorting with a cry for murder: "Crucify him! Crucify him!"

Where do we find ourselves at this station? When we get into groups, what do we yell and scream for? And what do we end up doing as members of crowds, nations, religious groups? There are choices: we can stand with those who incite others to violence, making it legal and getting what we want done, one way or another. We can stand with the crowd and taste blood, disappearing into the cover of the many who get sucked into revenge, destruction, racism, nationalism, killing for the sake of making a point, or just killing. We can stand with Pilate, waffling between what moves us personally but what is politically motivated, and expedite evil, making sure that we come out ahead no matter what might develop in a situation. Or we can just stand by and watch, waiting to see what happens, and then go home with the majority of people, feeling that the world is safer, or justice has been done, or someone got what they deserved, or their own need to exercise power in some form was served. Or, lastly, we can stand with Jesus and know that we will be handed over, and we will begin our agonizing death march.

This station is about politics, about nationalism and about self-interest and when and how we as religious people and religious institutions stand in collusion with the power of the state to further our own ends. There is in reality no separation of church and state. We either stand under the state's power and succumb to its methods and values, or we stand in opposition to them, serving the power of Jesus Christ the Crucified and following in Jesus' way of knowing when to speak, when to fall silent, when to resist with our very presence and lay our bodies on the line.

Arundhati Roy, an Indian writer, novelist, and community organizer, author of *The God of Small Things*, wrote in *The Nation* (February 18, 2002) something to take to heart at this station:

What we need to search for and find, what we need to hone and perfect into a magnificent, shining thing, is a new kind of politics. Not the politics of governance, but the politics of resistance. The politics of opposition. The politics of forcing accountability. The politics of slowing things down. The politics of joining hands across the world and preventing certain destruction. In the present circumstances, I'd say that the only thing worth globalizing is dissent.

There was no one to dissent, no other voice shouting out, no organizing to stop the killing and the injustice, all enacted according to the due process of the existing law and situation between an oppressive state and a fawning religious group, willing to use their hated enemy to further their own standing.

The Way of the Cross becomes harder with each station. The force and insidiousness of evil, as it spreads through personal relationships, groups, structures and institutions, nations and religions, only grows stronger and more violent. It is a spiral of violence that grows more degrading, more debilitating, more dehumanizing, drawing more people into its grip as it continues unabated, meeting no resistance. There is very little hope as Jesus and we who follow him face the ascent to the hill of Calvary and the actual crucifixion. This is the unfolding of the Scriptures and the killing of Jesus, but it is also the unfolding of reality in the world today and the escalation of the number of victims and the ferocity of those who practice state-craft, systems of economics based on profit and greed, and those who will do anything to maintain their positions in any group, even those who claim to live religious lives and worship God. There will be glimpses of hope, shards of refracted light at the Cross when Jesus is crucified, but on the way there is very little. Sobering, yet truthful. We are reminded that others who have sought hope and freedom have had to endure without much to go on, too.

Mohandas K. Gandhi wrote in a prison journal,

When I despair, I remember that all through history, the way
of truth and love has always won. There have been murderers
and tyrants, and for a time they can seem invincible. But in
the end they always fall. Think of it, always.

For followers, the Way of the Cross is shaped by the pattern of living
out our baptism promises: living in the freedom of the children of God.
Living with resistance to evil and refusing to be mastered by any sin.
Living under no sign of power but the sign of the cross, which means
living with integrity, nonviolence, justice, and love—loving as we have
been loved by God in Jesus, and willingly embracing our share of the
burden of the Gospel and the sufferings of the Cross. We must, with
Jesus, live reminding the world that we are human beings made in the
image of God and we cannot allow the sufferings and injustice of the
world to continue without protest. And while they do continue, we will
be found with those who know in their own flesh the suffering of injustice and sin, because we will be standing with Jesus hearing the cries
of a murderous crowd chanting, "Crucify him! Crucify him!"

Let us pray: Jesus, you stand silent, composed, being held together
by your faithfulness to your Father, knowing that you belong to God
completely. You will be his beloved child in suffering and death as you
have been in freedom and life. May we learn your fear only of failing
your Father and your integrity of resisting all that is not life-giving. In
the face of the world's injustice may we never be a part of attacking
others, expressing our rage against another human being or using our
religious identification and communities to validate any government or
group's vengeance, murder, or destruction. Teach us to stand humbly
before our God, knowing who we are, and to stand respectfully in the
presence of others. And deliver us from all harm. Amen.

The Sixth Station

■

JESUS IS SCOURGED
AND CROWNED
WITH THORNS

■

SCRIPTURE: JOHN 19:1–3

Pilate's next move was to take Jesus out and have him scourged. The soldiers then wove a crown of thorns and fixed it on his head, throwing around his shoulders a cloak of royal purple. Repeatedly they came up to him and said, "All hail, King of the Jews!", slapping his face as they did so.

Or

SCRIPTURE: MARK 15:16–20

The soldiers now led Jesus into the hall known as the praetorium; at the same time they assembled the whole cohort. They dressed him in royal purple, then wove a crown of thorns and put it on him, and began to salute him, "All hail! King of the Jews!" Continually striking Jesus on the head with a reed and spitting at him, they genuflected before him and pretended to pay him homage. When they had finished mocking him, they stripped him of the purple, dressed him in his own clothes, and led him out to crucify him.

■ ■ ■ ■ ■ ▩

The problem, unstated until now, is how to live in a damaged body in a world where pain is meant to be gagged uncured, ungrieved over. The problem is to connect, without hysteria, the pain of anyone's body with the pain of the world's body.

ADRIENNE RICH, POET

The way becomes fraught with horror. Now Jesus is utterly alone and handed over simply to be tortured, terrified, made sport of as immediate preparation for his grisly and ghastly public execution. But this is done away from the eyes of anyone who would care. They can do anything they want to him and no one will stop them. They will intentionally work on dehumanizing him, demeaning him, and instill in him a taste of what is to come, taking his dignity from him, piece by piece, as they take pieces of his skin and make him bleed, inflicting pain for the sake of inflicting pain.

These are soldiers, trained to hurt and kill. And the whole cohort is assembled to participate in the game. Jesus is led into the arena of war, of abuse, of torture, and the mindless inflicting of suffering. This is their turf, the praetorium, where they gathered to enjoy themselves and let off steam, where they got the chance to express their frustration and anger at being posted in this out-of-the-way country among a people that depised them. They taunt Jesus, mock him, strip him of his clothes and drape a purple cloak over his shoulders. They braid branches of a thick thornbush into a roughly formed crown and push it down into his scalp, making sure it's good and secure. They take turns coming before him, spitting, genuflecting and making fun of him, insulting him, and hitting him in the face and on the head.

They are all faceless. They are a cohort. They are not individuals. They are intent only on trying to destroy this one man. There is only one individual here, the man Jesus who seeks to hold on to his body and soul in the face of such inhumanity. This ordeal all began with Judas's kiss, at which time his heart would have begun to crack and break. With each person who turns from him—Peter, the disciples, strangers who would take a bribe to bear false witness against him, the leaders and elders of his own religion who have relentlessly sought to have him destroyed out of hate and jealousy—with each of them another piece of his heart would shatter and the pain would seep through his soul.

And now the sleep deprivation, the trials and interrogation, his own knowledge of the brutal death penalty that he faces would begin to take its toll on his body. There is no specific description of the scourging, the flogging, that he received, but accounts of it in Roman histories are almost unbearable even to read. Basically there were thirty-nine lashes (no more or most would die from the wounds) administered with a whip that had ten or twelve lashes, each tipped with pieces of metal or glass. It would be slow, methodical, well-practiced and was designed to reduce the person being beaten to a mass of open flesh, hanging tissue and nerves, multiple wounds inches deep delivered thirty-nine times. No mercy. When it was done, it was done. And they would have turned and gone on with the preparations for the next step in the execution. It is unbelievable the amount of hate the human body can sustain before it begins to break.

We are horrified when we think of what was done to Jesus. But are we equally horrified when this is done to others? Jesus was alone, without protection, defense, or recourse, as are so many hundreds of thousands of human beings today. These atrocities are practiced in the world today, in prisons, interrogation centers, among governments and groups so angry and frustrated that they engage in torture and destruction as a way of dealing with their political and economic situations. We haven't found ways to stop such practices. We have groups like Amnesty International and Human Rights Watch and Pax Christi that seek to speak of what is happening, to keep the public aware of the horrors that occur routinely in the name of democracy and homeland security. There are centers that train others to do it worldwide, funded and staffed by military officers, troops and educators that share such information across borders with those who will use it to their advantage, complying with the more aggressive nations' demand that they control groups within their borders. It is done here in the United States with other countries' military in wars against drugs, peasants, labor unions and organizers, religious missionaries and churches that resist and preach peace with justice. But we must not look away, or we will be in jeopardy of losing our own humanity.

Contemplating the suffering which is unbearable to us, and is
unbearable to others, too, can produce awake mind, which
arises from the compassion that wishes to free all living beings
from suffering.

(DALAI LAMA)

When the range and depth of the sufferings of others and what we
do to one another no longer bothers us, nor moves us to remedy the situation and stop the pain, then we have lost a part of our own humanity,
our own soul. Such sufferings must bother us, and we must speak of
them and firmly resolve to find ways to eliminate them from our world.
Each time we do not act, do not speak, they grow in horror and scope
and they come home to be expressed among us, in our families, our
schools, and our churches.

The abuse in families, children dying as a result of parental rage
and impatience, spousal abuse, and the torture of the elderly are bred
of the same callousness of the torturer. The teasing, insulting, exclud-
ing, and humiliating of students, the inflicting of pain, are learned from
watching it practiced as the national and international way of reacting
to others who frighten us and whom we feel we cannot control and so
must kill.

The Stations of the Cross could just as clearly be called the stations of justice, or the way of justice. Each station, each confrontation
between Jesus and another person or a group, reveals what we do to
each other, personally and on a public level. Each station is an indict-
ment against Christians, followers of the man crucified, the suffering
servant, the Lamb of God, who insists that we look at him and so look
at ourselves and decide: will we follow the Way of the Cross, or will we
follow the way of violence and intimidation, murder and divisions? Are
we the presence of God in the world, or do we bow to the world's
frightening attempts to silence truth and justice for all the children of
God?

We are human and so we know pain, as we know birth and death, but there is suffering that no human being should have to experience. This suffering is inflicted by others, needlessly, repeatedly, unmindful of any relation to the other as human, rationalized and sometimes blessed by a group, fueled by fear, indignation, insecurity, and nationalistic and religious arrogance. And Jesus knew this suffering. He faced it and in his life and suffering and dying by crucifixion he showed us how to live with it, and live in such a way that we spend our lives relieving it, atoning for it, trying to prevent it, and when it cannot be escaped, uniting it with his own. We proclaim, "I have been crucified with Christ . . . I carry the brand marks of Christ in my body." (Galatians 2:20; 6:17) We must look at the scourging and mutilation of the Crucified One among us. Canadian theologian Douglas John Hall writes,

> Until such a mutilated, sorrowful, forsaken Christ can be met
> in the churches of suburbia, there will be no facing up to the
> mutiliation, sorrow, and forsakenness that this continent and
> its European satellites visit upon millions of the poor, includ-
> ing our own poor. Nor will there be any confrontation with the
> sickness within the soul of this society which causes it to seek
> the enemy outside its own soul.
>
> (LIGHTEN OUR DARKNESS: TOWARDS AN INDIGENOUS THEOLOGY OF
> THE CROSS [PHILADELPHIA: WESTMINSTER PRESS, 1976], PP. 140–41.)

The antidote for this kind of suffering inflicted upon others, either individually, in state-sponsored torture, or in the economically sanctioned starvation and destruction of a peoples' resources and land, lies in the foundation of religion: adoration and worship. This kind of suffering that so scars the face of humanity and the earth is sacrilege, for what we do to one another our God takes as done to the Body of the Beloved Child Jesus. We must be converted to seeing our God in the bodies of all peoples. It is a way of life devoted to both prayer and practice, alone and with others.

Let us pray with Thomas Merton:

Oh God, in accepting one another wholeheartedly, fully, completely, we accept You, and we thank You, and we adore You, and we love You with our whole being, because our being is in Your being, our spirit is rooted in Your spirit. Fill us then with love, and let us be bound together with love as we go our diverse ways, united in this one spirit which makes You present in the world, and which makes You witness to the ultimate reality that is love. Love has overcome. Love is victorious. Amen.

(THOMAS MERTON'S CLOSING PRAYER AT THE FIRST SPIRITUAL
SUMMIT CONFERENCE IN CALCUTTA, INDIA; QUOTED IN PATRICK
HART, NAOMI BURTON STONE, JAMES LAUGHLIN, EDS., *THE ASIAN
JOURNAL OF THOMAS MERTON* [NEW YORK: W.W. NORTON, 1988],
PP. 318–319)

The Seventh Station

■

JESUS
CARRIES
HIS CROSS

■

SCRIPTURE: JOHN 19:17

Jesus was led away and, carrying his cross by himself, went out to what is called the Place of the Skull (in Hebrew, Golgotha).

Or

SCRIPTURE: MARK 15:20

When they had finished mocking him, they stripped him of the purple, dressed him in his own clothes, and led him out to crucify him.

■ ■ ■ ■ ■ ■

If then, you are looking for the way by which you should go, take Christ, because he himself is the way.

THOMAS AQUINAS

Just one line. The stations grow shorter. Jesus is led out, like a lamb to the slaughter, sacrificed by people. It is the reverse of the Exodus, when the people were led out of bondage into freedom. Now once again the slaughter begins. We are the people of the Cross. We are marked with the sign of the cross in every ritual of the catechumentate that prepares adults for baptism. We begin every prayer and liturgy in the sign of the cross. We bless, we pray, we anoint, we even do it unthinkingly as we pass by churches, cemeteries, and before we board planes or face moments of decision and fear. The Way of the Cross begins at baptism. This marking people with a sign, usually on the forehead, was an ancient Jewish practice. In the book of Ezekiel, the prophet placed a mark (an X) on those who mourned and groaned over the abominations that were practiced in the city of Jerusalem. All those without the mark were to be struck down and shown no mercy. This is an echo of the blood mark on the doorposts of the Israelites as the Angel of Death passed through Egypt, sparing those with the sign of deliverance. (Ezekiel 9:1–6) And in the Book of Revelation the vision of the angels ravaging the land and the sea is preceded by "an angel holding the seal of the living God." The command was given: "Do no harm to the land or the sea or the trees until we imprint this seal on the foreheads of the servants of our God" (Rev. 7:2–3). With this mark we commit ourselves to being led out to be crucified with Jesus, our Lord.

The Cross has religious meaning that draws us into the community of the Trinity and marks us with the values of nonviolence, forgiveness, mercy, love unto death, bearing our share of the burden of the Gospel, picking up and helping others to carry their crosses, filling up what is lacking in the sufferings of Christ, peacemaking and reconciling among all factions, healing divisions and working for unity. Because of the power and strength of the cross, it challenges every other power on the face of the earth, and so it has come to have a strong political meaning as well.

Throughout history the cross stands as a symbol of protest and revolt; protest against all claims, whether by religious or political power, to absolute unquestioning control over human minds and bodies; revolt against all systems and ideologies, all regimes and institutions, which continue to push individuals and groups beyond the pale, outside the gate. The cross stands as a symbol of the falsehood and demonic nature of all religions which sanctify established injustice, religions of the *status quo*, which continue to reproduce Calvaries all over the world. The cross is a crisis point for all societies which seek to produce men and women of quiescence, men and women who are trained to give unquestioning, uncritical obedience to worldly powers and not to Christ; a crisis point for all systems of violence, systems which are bound to lead to the reproduction of Calvaries great and small; a crisis point for all who despise the weak and the small people, and in so doing despise Christ.

(KENNETH LEECH, *WE PREACH CHRIST CRUCIFIED: THE PROCLAMATION OF THE CROSS IN A DARK AGE* [LONDON: DARTON, LONGMAN AND TODD, 1994], p. 51)

Jesus came preaching good news to the poor, living with them, dying with them, and raising their plight and existence to a level of solidarity with himself and all his followers. When a young man of property and possessions approached Jesus about sharing in everlasting life and he was questioned on his obedience to the law, Jesus responds generously, graciously offering him a place in his own company of followers. "Jesus looked at him with love and told him, 'There is one thing more you must do. Go and sell what you have and give it to the poor: you will then have treasure in heaven. After that, come and follow me.' And at these words the man's face fell. He went away sad, for he had many possessions." (Mk. 10:21–22) What a pity! He turned down intimacy with God, a family bound in the word and will of his Father and the company of brothers and sisters struggling to bring the kingdom of justice and peace upon earth now. Since then, this call to poverty, to care and solidarity with the poor, has been seen as difficult, as impossible, or as a blessing and an unequivocal necessity in following Jesus. We are exhorted to become sensitive to the needs of others as part of our spirituality in words such as these from Louis Guanella: "The heart of a Christian, who believes and feels, cannot pass by the hardships and deprivations of the poor without helping them." And we are severely warned by the theologian Robert Bellarmine that

> The superfluous riches which thou dist hoard and suffer to become rotten when thou shouldst have given them in alms to the poor, the superfluous garments which thou didst possess and preferred to see eaten by moths rather than clothing the poor, and the gold and silver which thou didst choose to see lie in idleness rather than spent on food for the poor, all these things, I say, will bear testimony against thee in the day of Judgment.

The poor carry the cross all the time, and Jesus carries all the poor. He has made them his cause in the world, knowing the burden laid on them by economic injustices and inequality, and the greed and sin of others—individuals, corporations, and countries. But in this age of the millenium the issue of poverty is global in its proportions and like a dry tree in the path of a wild fire waiting to explode and add fuel to the fire as it continues in its ceaseless destruction. The poverty, starvation, and desperation of more than six-tenths of the world's population has become a root evil that feeds violence, hatred, terrorism, and nationalism.

In a Vatican address at the United Nations on the subject of disarmament by Archbishop Renato Martino, the Vatican's permanent observer at the United Nations, in a paper called "Unjust Status Quo Will Continue Fueling Conflicts," he wrote,

Any serious campaign against terrorism needs to address the social, economic and political conditions that nuture the emergence of terrorism.

The most dramatic example of inequality is the growing gap between the rich and poor. The north, containing a fifth of the world population, controls 80 percent of the wealth and resources; the south, with four-fifths of the world population, has only 20 percent of the wealth and resources. This is not only unjust; it is a threat to the stability of the planet. It is the determination of the strong to maintain their position by whatever means necessary, whether military, financial or political, which is the basis for the systemic inequality in the world. A commitment to equity in the world is the only secure foundation for a more humane world order. Nations must work together to blunt current disparities and improve global stability. A continuation of the unjust status quo will inevitably continue fueling conflicts and will lead to even more conflicts in the decades ahead.

People are poor most often because of larger issues that impact their work, their families, their lands and crops. Jesus came preaching an ethic and a spirituality that was based on sharing, on justice for all, on jubilee justice that included redistribution of land to those without, a sabbath schedule for the canceling of debts that were impossible to pay, of providing immigrants, migrants, and the poor with seed and safety on their own land or a welcome within Israel; the freeing of slaves and indentured servants, the release of prisoners, so that there was a foundation of hope built into the economic and political system. But he went much farther. The poor were his own, his friends and neighbors. They were held up for high praise, and his disciples were told to observe how they lived, as when he watched with care the widow who put her small pittance in the temple treasure, giving out of her very sustenance to survive. In fact, he compared himself to such impoverished, generous, and gracious people, for he himself would give everything he had, even his

very life so that others might know life. Today the core of holiness is hos-
pitality to the poor, an ethic of sharing and of the necessity to live as
simply as we can so that others might simply live, coupled with the imperative of justice for the majority of the world, which is denied the basic necessities of life by businesses, international monetary funds,
banks, and global corporations. Jesus lived in occupied territory, in
poverty and misery, and his stories and preaching are all about food,
land, liberation from bondage and servitude and debt. He preached
about providing for those who lacked the most and were considered expendable, as the birds of the air, and yet in Jesus' eyes were where one
found the treasure of heaven, here, now, on earth.

There was a story told by Hal Brady during the Boer War about
William Booth, who founded the Salvation Army. Some very hungry
people gathered to discuss how to distribute a small amount of food. It
was understood that each church was supposed to take care of its own.
The local Episcopal rector said, "My church, follow me." The Presby-
terian minister said, "Mine, follow me." And the other denominations
did the same. There were a lot of folks left. Then William Booth
stepped forward and said: "All of you who belong to nobody, you
follow me."

Jesus bears his cross and walks through the city, climbs Calvary to
die in the garbage dump outside the city walls, as poor as one can become in this world. He carries his cross, the burden laid on him by a
oppressive occupying force that sought to steal the food, crops, land,
and labor of his own people, a religious structure seeking only to better
its own position and privileged lifestyle, taxing its own already heavily
burdened people. These oppressors cared more about their possessions
than about people's bodies and souls. We bear our cross.

Let us pray: Poor Jesus, may all we have and all we are belong to
you. Feel free to share it around, to break it up as you broke bread and
pour it out in cups of wine that are filled with the rich blood of your
new family of all those who belong to nobody, nobody except you and
those who are of your company. Amen.

The Eighth Station

■

JESUS IS HELPED
BY SIMON
OF CYRENE

■

SCRIPTURE: MARK 15:20–21

When they had finished mocking him, they stripped him of the purple, dressed him in his own clothes, and led him out to crucify him. A man named Simon of Cyrene, the father of Alexander and Rufus, was coming in from the fields, and they pressed him into service to carry the cross.

Or

SCRIPTURE: LUKE 23:26

As they led him away, they laid hold of one Simon the Cyrenian who was coming in from the fields. They put a crossbeam on Simon's shoulders for him to carry along behind Jesus.

■ ■ ■ ■ ■ ■

Our only hope today lies in our ability to recapture the revolutionary spirit and go out into a sometimes hostile world declaring eternal hostility to poverty, racism, and militarism.

MARTIN LUTHER KING, JR.

We are halfway through the stations, and this eighth station is a hinge, where the focus begins to shift. In the first half, the eye is on Jesus and what he does. Now there is a subtle shift toward us and what we do in relation to Jesus, whether we chose to be with, help, reject, watch, or harm. Here again the reading is short, but we have names: Simon of Cyrene, traditionally a black laborer, and the names of his two children, Rufus and Alexander, and we know nothing else about the three of them. Traditionally, if you are named you are actually a member of the community, known and trustworthy. Simon is remembered because of what he does for Jesus, but perhaps he is remembered as well because his children are Christians because of what he did for Jesus. We wonder, will our children be Christians because of what we do today in the world?

He is coming in from the fields, on his way home, or elsewhere, but he is not a part of the proceedings. He may not even know who Jesus is; he walks into a mob, an execution, and is pressed into service. He does not belong to any of the political or religious factions, yet his life will be radically altered forever because of a chance encounter with a condemned man carrying a cross. He helps Jesus under duress, probably thinking he had the bad luck to be in the wrong place at the wrong time. Simon is most probably poor, a farmer, day laborer, someone else's hired hand, but suddenly he is yanked down another rung or two on the ladder of society. This is downward mobility forced on him, and the beam is laid across his shoulders to bear, and he falls in behind Jesus, who is in much worse a position than he is, thinking, Why me? And yet he is remembered for carrying the burden of God, for God.

The beam laid across his shoulders makes him an image of the Crucified himself. For us, we can remember Jesus' words: "Come to me all you who are weary and heavy burdened, and I will refresh you. Take my yoke upon your shoulders and learn from me, for I am gentle and humble of heart. Your souls will find rest, for my yoke is easy and my burden light." (Mt. 11:28–30) The word *yoke* has a number of meanings. First, it is the yoke holding two animals or slaves together so that together they can do more work, more quickly than they could separately, leaning into each other and supporting one another. Second, it means the yoke of the cross carried as a slave would carry the burden pole of clay or water pots. And third, it evokes the image of men and women with their arms thrown across each others' shoulders, as is done in many countries, while they dance! Simon now knows all these meanings in the experience of being pressed into the service of helping Jesus. His terrible burden will be the doorway to his future, radically changed, and his entrance into the kingdom of justice and peace.

More amazingly, he will bear the burden of God for a while, and in exchange he will be forever remembered as the image of the disciple on the Way. This is Simon of Cyrene as opposed to Simon Peter, who has rejected in anger and fear any possibility of aiding his Master on the road to Calvary. This is Simon Nobody as opposed to Simon the leader of the disciples, the head of the church. When all others leave, it is nobody who falls in behind Jesus on his way.

We, too, are pressed into service along with Simon, often under duress. Massive human need draws the Simons of the world into homeless shelters, soup kitchens, back alleys, refugee camps, and endless lines of people waiting for food, tents, medicine. We are usually reluctant to be associated with the poor, the victims, the condemned, those who could be a threat to our security, those of other races and cultures. Traditionally, Simon of Cyrene is believed to have been black, easily chosen out of a crowd, an outsider, a stranger. He fell into the moment that would save him. James Baldwin wrote in 1961, "There is never time in the future in which we will work out our salvation. The challenge is in the moment, the time is always now." And he shared in another's burden, echoing Maya Angelou's words in 1986: "Prejudice is a burden which confuses the past, threatens the future, and renders the present inaccessible." It is notable that the one person who is named, honored, and remembered in this agonizing walk of justice and pain is of another race. Without thought of such things, he lives another of James Baldwin's lines: "Isn't love more important than color?"

(1963) Sadly, he also declares the truth of Langston Hughes's saying that "there is no color line in death" (1945).

Two thousand years later, racism is a cross many are pressured into bearing, considered to be in the wrong place at the wrong time, poor and easily drawn into the downward spiral of violence and systemic evil. Today many people of color in the United States feel that their burden is growing heavier and that much of what was secured in the past is slipping away again. And that now there are even harder issues to face. Listen to some people speak of their cross and burden today.

> The masses of our people recognize that most of the defining issues of the Civil Rights Movement *no longer exist*. We face an unprecedented crisis of poverty, violence, joblessness, and social despair, and the old approaches are no longer sufficient or viable.
>
> (MANNING MARABLE, 1997)

> I almost weep when I see what has happened to the civil rights movement, the bloody struggles for racial justice. . . . So much that was won over the bites of police dogs, the truncheons of bigoted cops, has been diluted—or lost.
>
> (CARL T. ROWAN, 1991)

> Two hundred and forty-four years of slavery and nearly a century of institutionalized terrorism in the form of segregation, lynchings, and second-class citizenship in America . . . has left its toll in the psychic scars and personal wounds now inscribed in the souls of black folk.
>
> (CORNEL WEST, 1993)

When we speak of racism, much of our history is framed within the context of the sin of slavery, but racism overlaps in the histories and experiences of the indigenous people of this continent, the Hispanic-

Latino and wave after wave of immigrants from countries of the southern hemispheres. More recently the blanket of racism is thrown wider to include people of Eastern European, Central Asian, and Arabic descent, language, and religion. This expansion to include so many new groups of people becomes a burden that is more complex and interrelated than the previous one.

> Immigrants from Africa, Asia and the Pacific, Central and
> Latin America and the Caribbean, have made the "minority"
> population increasingly diverse. . . . The politics of divide and
> rule set one group against another, and encourage them to
> fight for the ever smaller pieces of the American pie reserved
> for people who are neither white, nor well off.
>
> (PROJECT HIP-HOP, 1997)

In an ever more technological world that brings together continents and time zones so that we know what is happening within minutes or hours half a world away, the issue of racism is surfacing as a subject for misunderstanding as deeply divisive and morally reprehensible as that of nationalism, its ethical cousin. Yet the underlying answer is ancient, foundational, and human. Sara Harrington reminds us of what we so often forget:

> While the legal, material and even superficial requirements to
> eradicate racism are well known, its psychological and more
> deeply spiritual requirements have been persistently neg-
> lected—namely, the oneness of the human family. It is this
> principle of oneness that needs to be the driving force behind
> the struggle of uniting the races.
>
> (1998)

This station is short, and intensely, personally, to the point in the midst of a violent structural reality. It begins with the reporting that "they stripped him of the purple cloak and put his own clothes on him." Purple is the color of kings, of the military commander, representing power over others, and they use it to mock Jesus, who has preached a kingdom of reconciliation, peace with justice, where all share their goods according to the needs of others. Jesus has called his followers to be a kingdom based on the power of service, of being the ransom for many and the alternative to "the lording over it" of the world. We are to be the servant of all, and as leaders we are to be the servants of God.

It is time to decide whether or not we will fall in behind Simon of Cyrene and bear one another's burdens, to not only be pressed into service, but to volunteer for it and actively recruit others to follow in Jesus' footsteps. Perhaps it is time to look around and see who needs help, who needs a burden lifted, who needs to know that they are not alone, discarded, or scorned. This attitude may mean coming down a step or two in our socioeconomic status, but it may also mean that another is brought up that step or two, so that we walk together again.

Let us pray: Jesus, you are our God, who walks ahead of us hoping that we will fall in behind you. May we be drawn into your presence, like Simon, even reluctantly, and accept the crosses that are pressed upon us. May we look upon one another with the eyes of gratitude and respect, as you must have looked upon Simon. May your faithfulness and your acceptance of us in your becoming one of us give us the courage to reach out to all, across borders and boundaries of color, culture, language, religion, and economics. And someday may we throw out our arms over each others' shoulders and know the dance of life and communion. Amen.

(Note: all quotes in this station are from "And Don't Call Me a Racist!": A Treasury of Quotes on the Past, Present and Future of the Color Line in America, selected and arranged by Ella Mazel (Lexington, Mass.: Argonaut Press, 1998).

The Ninth Station

■

JESUS ENCOUNTERS
THE WOMEN
OF JERUSALEM

■

SCRIPTURE: LUKE 23:27–31

A great crowd of people followed him, including women who beat their breasts and lamented over him. Jesus turned to them and said, "Daughters of Jerusalem, do not weep for me. Weep for your-selves and for your children. The days are coming when they will say, 'Happy are the sterile, the wombs that never bore and the breasts that never nursed.' Then they will begin saying to the mountains, 'Fall on us,' and to the hills, 'Cover us.' If they do these things in the green wood, what will happen in the dry?"

■　■　■　■　■　■

Your children will have to live with ours.

AN IRAQI TEACHER BEFORE SEPTEMBER 11th

Jesus draws closer to the place of his execution, and there are many women in the crowd, wailing, crying out, weeping, and lamenting over him. One would think that Jesus would be grateful for their expression of compassion for his condition, but instead he turns toward them and reprimands them, deflecting their tears away from him and redirecting their emotions. There are two kinds of lamentations: the cries of the women weeping for him that are dead ends. They are emotionally charged, beating their breasts in a frenzy of mourning, but they do not result in action. Nothing changes, and the Way of the Cross, the killing, the inflicting of pain on innocent people, and the torture continue. And then there are the lamentations, the cries and tears of the prophets. Even while on his way to his death, Jesus is the teacher, the prophet, the Word of God made flesh, Emmanuel among us.

We know only two instances of Jesus' own tears and lamentation. He wept for his beloved Lazarus who died without his presence and comfort when he was told to "Lord, come and see" in response to his question of where they had laid him. (Jn. 11:34). This incidence was more than just mourning the death of his friend, because in the very first chapter of the Gospel of John, Jesus is asked by the two disciples who come after him, where he lives, and he uses these same words: "Come and see" (Jn. 1:39). These words were their invitation to life, to enter into Jesus' presence and his dwelling with God, to share where he lived. Now, near the end of his life he is being told to come and see where death reigns, where everyone believes life ends. They have not heard of, or learned about, or come to believe in life. Death still pervades their lives—and so much of ours as well.

The other time we know of that Jesus wept was when he mourned and lamented over a whole city, Jerusalem—a people, a nation, and its history—because they missed his coming, his message, and his presence as justice and peace among them. The account is one of a prophet's lamentation, a prophet's tears of anger, of the frustration of God, calling his people to change, now, before it is too late.

Coming within sight of the city, he wept over it and said, "If only you had known the path to peace this day; but you have completely lost it from view! Days will come upon you when your enemies encircle you with a rampart, hem you in, and press you hard from every side. They will wipe you out, you and your children within your walls, and not leave a stone on a stone within you, because you failed to recognize the time of your visitation."

(LUKE 19:41–44)

A prophet is one who sees so clearly what is happening and being done in the present that they can tell us what will happen to us if we do not change now, immediately, turning from our present course. This has been Jesus' calling, and even as he draws near to facing his own death for his words of truth-telling, he still speaks to anyone he passes along the way. There is a weeping that is cathartic for the person who cries but is useless and allows the destruction on the cross to continue. In this case, no one moves to help Jesus or even to stand with him. But there is another type of weeping and lamentation that leads to conversion, to the work for justice, the easing of pain and the giving of hope to those in desperate despair and need.

Jesus is trying to tell them that his death, anyone's death like this has massive ramifications for the future, and for the future of our children. Compassion for the sufferings of others should be translated into conversion and transformation of reality. When we walk the Way of the Cross with Jesus we want to weep over what was done to Jesus, but Jesus does not want us to get caught up in this kind of emotionalism and self-absorbed devotion. He is concerned that we do something, for ourselves and for our children. When children learn that their parents were there, in places where they witnessed suffering, and did not do anything, what will they think? If nothing is done to stop this kind of legal killing, this governmental and military control over oppressed peoples, this state-sanctioned and brutal torture, what will be the fate of our children? And Jesus tries to warn them prophetically that it will be worse, and continue to worsen until we turn our tears into the hard work of justice, telling the truth and turning the world back to being human.

A more contemporary prophet wrote disturbing words over fifty years ago to a world community dealing with the problems of racism, nationalism, colonialism, slavery, inequality, religious fanaticism, and militarism in violent ways:

> What does it matter to the dead, the orphans, and the home-
> less whether the mad destruction is wrought under the name
> of totalitarianism or the holy name of liberty or democracy?
>
> (MAHATMA GANDHI)

The problems are immense and worldwide, but the response to them makes or breaks us as human beings. Eleanor Roosevelt wrote, "When will our consciences grow so tender that we will act to prevent human misery rather than avenge it?" What we do affects the present but creates a foundation of hate, injustice, and revenge for generations to come. And it affects children everywhere, now and in the future. This e-mail message circulated just after the events of September 11th:

> *On September 11, 2001, 36,000 children worldwide died of hunger.*
> *Where: Poor countries.*
> *News stories: none.*
> *Newspaper articles: none.*
> *Military alerts: none.*
> *Presidential proclamations: none.*
> *Papal messages: none.*
> *Messages of solidarity: none.*
> *Minutes of silence: none.*
> *Homage to the innocent children: none.*

The larger statistics are even more disturbing. In the past six years about 25,000 people have died from terrorist attacks worldwide. In that same period of time—six years—55 million people, about 25,000 a day, have died from preventable starvation. In war, in poverty, in conflicts, it is the children who know the pain first and are the first to die, the most to die.

There is an old Jewish story told of a rabbi whose child suddenly became desperately ill. So many people were anxious for his welfare. There was an outpouring of cards, letters, prayers, services held for the child. There was an endless stream of visitors bringing food, drink, medicines, and doctors, the most expert in their field. And the child recovered. Everyone expected the rabbi to be overjoyed, ecstatic, but instead they found him weeping uncontrollably. They questioned him and his answer surprised them. He said, "When my child was sick there was so much concern, care, tears, prayers, and everyone did what they could until he was well again. All I could think about was the horrifying reality that if it is anyone else's child that gets sick, there isn't much concern shown. No one offers free medicines, care, food, changing their lives to make sure that everything is done so that this child lives. Is my child any more precious than any other child in this town or country, or anywhere? That is why I weep. Someone must weep over all the children lost, unmourned, uncared for and left to fend for themselves."

Jesus' suffering is terrible, but we continue to destroy one another, beginning with the children, everywhere by means of our wars, greed, economic policies (such as a complex two-year limit on welfare benefits), immigration laws that deny children health care, enlisting of children as soldiers, allowing child labor practices and even child slavery, allowing children to live without clean water or adequate food, suffering the loss of their parents, in the midst of violence and poverty. Jesus tells us to weep not for him, but for ourselves and what we continue to do to each other and how we put the children of the world in jeopardy. He tells us to then do something about it: now! Consider these children's rights:

I HAVE THE RIGHT . . .

To life, with all its joys and struggles;

To responsible, mature, and loving parents;

To an education that promotes my self-esteem and identity as a unique human being, a member of a family and a nation;

To nutrition, health care, and a safe environment;

To protection from armed and social violence, including toys, games, and entertainments that promote violence;

To be protected from exploitation and abuse, whether physical, sexual, emotional, or psychological;

To know my own culture and traditions;

To be heard by parents, teachers, politicans, police, and clergy;

To protection from discrimination of any sort.

(ADAPTED FROM THE UN CONVENTION ON THE RIGHTS OF THE CHILD)

It is time to stop our weeping and beating of breasts and getting emotional over the state of affairs in the world and the sufferings of others, especially children, and move—do something that will convert our lives and transform the lives of those who come after us, down to the seventh generation, as the indigenous people of this country teach. No more tears without accompanying action—otherwise the future will turn and condemn us for our inaction and our selfishness.

Let us pray: Jesus, teach us how to weep and lament as you did, as prophets and people dedicated to honoring the God who made us by caring for the least among us, beginning with all the children of the earth. Teach us how to be their shield and protection, their safety and their refuge, so that they do not live in fear, in need, and without hope for a future. Jesus, may all who encounter us on our Way of the Cross, know that we care for them by our actions and our resistance to all unnecessary pain, not just words or tears. Whenever we weep, Oh Lord, let the tears wash clear our eyes and stir us to make "justice roll like a river" for the children and those who come after us in faith. Amen.

The Tenth Station

∎

JESUS

IS

CRUCIFIED

∎

SCRIPTURE: MARK 15:22–26

When they brought Jesus to the site of Golgotha (which means "Skull Place"), they tried to give him wine drugged with myrrh, but he would not take it. Then they crucified him and divided up his garments by rolling dice for them to see what each would take. It was about nine in the morning when they crucified him. The inscription proclaiming his offense read, "The King of the Jews."

Or

SCRIPTURE: LUKE 23:32–34

Two others who were criminals were led along with him to be crucified. When they came to the Skull Place, as it was called, they crucified him there and the criminals as well, one on his right and the other on his left. Jesus said, "Father, forgive them; they do not know what they are doing." They divided his garments, rolling dice for them.

■ ■ ■ ■ ■

Love him totally who gave himself totally for your love.

CLAIRE OF ASSISI

Jesus is nailed to the crossbeam, and then it is lifted up and dropped into position with his writhing body attached to it. It begins. A slow death agony. There are only three words: they crucified him. And yet we are immediately directed to what is going on around him. They are on the ground below him. He hangs above them, struggling to breathe, his body a sheath of pain. And they're dividing the spoils; taking home souvenirs, acting like animals—scavengers, oblivious to what is happening to this human being they have just nailed to wood. They are grabbing what they can for themselves, uncaring of the pain they have just inflicted. Jesus is hours from death, but he is the only one truly alive in this scene, this station. The executioners are just referred to as "they"—nameless, faceless, without identities or soul, utterly insensitive to anything that does not concern them. And it's all legal, but inhuman and unjust.

This moment is about being a human being. And the soldiers, because that is who they are, fail miserably. What constitutes being a human being? In the Book of Exodus there is a line that is startling and descriptive. The story of Moses being rescued from the reeds and raised in Pharaoh's household jumps from that rescue to Moses seeing, witnessing, the forced labor and the sufferings of his people, and we are told abruptly that "Moses grew up" (Ex. 2:11). The essence of a mature human being in religious terms is this ability to see, to be aware of others' suffering and to be touched by it.

Jesus is being butchered and left to hang like a piece of meat nailed to pieces of wood, and those who did it are interested only in what little he had, his clothes. Now he has absolutely nothing. He is naked, vulnerable, bleeding from multiple wounds, and his skin is in shreds from the scourging. All he can do is try to breathe and to endure, and yet he is aware of everything. He is trusting in God and clinging to him still. His words are astounding in any situation; in this one of approaching death and torture, they are shattering. He prays forgiveness for those who have done this to him, for all people, for us, because we do not know what we are doing. The essence of being human

is having concern, sensitivity to others' needs and pain, and the ultimate act of that concern is to offer forgiveness to others. This practice
of forgiveness is the heart of our religion, our discipleship as individuals, as a church and as human beings. There are only two choices in
this station: to be human, made in the image of God, with Jesus; or to
be inhuman, consumed with greed and unaware of the pain that is inflicted upon others. Put in simple options, it is to be human and forgive, make peace in spite of all hatred, or to be inhuman and kill,
dividing the spoils. To be dead before you die. This is war reduced
down to its essentials.

When will we learn? We are told by many that this is the state of
affairs and these are our choices.

> I know war as few other men now living know it, and nothing
> to me is more revolting. I have long advocated its complete
> abolition, as its very destructiveness on both friend and foe has
> rendered it useless as a method of settling international dis-
> putes.
>
> (DOUGLAS MACARTHUR)

There is a story told today about the Women in Black and their
long devotion and action to promote peace between the Jews and the
Arabs in Israel, and to witness against the occupation. They are mainly
Israeli Jewish women, though it is hard to tell because they wear the
long chadors of the Palestinian women, and they station themselves at
the wailing wall every Sabbath evening. They vigil and they gather to
pray. First they pray Kaddish, the prayer of mourning for the dead, for
all the Israelis who have died that week, and then again Kaddish for all
the Palestinians who have died. They endure insults and curses, being
spit on and sometimes stoned, but they come every week. This has
been going on for years. Just recently an Israeli mother whose daughter
was killed by a suicide bomber addressed the group: "For me, the other
side, the enemy, is not the Palestinian people. For me the struggle is

not between Palestinians and Israelis, nor between Jews and Arabs. There are only two kinds of people in the world: those who seek peace and those who seek war. My people are those who seek peace."

On a very pragmatic level the Vatican has issued a statement (dated November 12, 2001) that was delivered to the United Nations calling for an end immediately to all nuclear testing, to honor the existing treaties worldwide, to decommission weapons, and certainly not to pursue the creation of newer ones.

> The Holy See, convinced that the time has come for the world to end all nuclear weapons testing for all time, wishes to add its voice of support to all efforts to ensure the entry into force of the Comprehensive Test Ban Treaty (CTBT).
>
> Having signed the CTBT on 24 September 1996, the Holy See deposited the Instrument of Ratification on 18 July 2001, reiterating the firm conviction that nuclear weapons are incompatible with the peace we seek for the twenty-first century; they cannot be justified. Those weapons are instruments of death and destruction.
>
> The Holy See is convinced that in the sphere of nuclear weapons, the banning of tests and the further development of these weapons, disarmament and non-proliferation are closely linked and must be achieved as quickly as possible under effective international controls. Today the Holy See adds its voice to those who appeal to the states whose ratification is necessary for the entry into force of the treaty.

(Note: the United States has not signed the treaty and has withdrawn from the Anti-Ballistic Missile Treaty [ABTM] and refused to join the nations of the World Court in supporting the Children Soldiers Treaty, the Banning of Landmines Treaty, and the Kyoto Environmental Agreement, or to participate as a member of the World Court.)

If we stop at this station and look upon the Crucified One hanging

before us and then at the soldiers rolling dice below, we must chose
which side we will live on. We must stand and begin the litany of death
and destruction occurring around the world along with the wounds of
the past and those of the future. Japan, China, Russia, Vietnam, Cam-
bodia, Nicaragua, El Salvador, Guatemala, Chiapas Mexico, Columbia,
Peru, Chile, East Timor, the Moluccas, Sudan, Iraq, Iran, Somalia, the
Congo, Rwanda, Sierre Leone, Israel/Palestine, Kurdistan, Northern
Ireland, Bosnia, and Serbia are some of the more persistent areas of
conflict. Distortions of fundamentalism and fanaticism in religion and
nationalism; terrorism; military incursions for economic greed; biological, chemical and nuclear weapons; sanctions against entire peoples are
how we nail one another to the cross, crucifying our God again and
again.

We must remember that we are a peaceful church, a community of
peacemakers, disciples of peace, representing the person of Christ, his
presence in the world. There is a story told of Pope John XXIII. He in-
vited representatives from seventy-five nations and more than a dozen
international organizations to a special audience when he first become
Pope—in fact, the day after the opening of the Vatican Council. They
were received in the magnificence of the newly restored Sistine Chapel
in front of Michelangelo's fresco, *The Last Judgment.* He addressed
them passionately, and at the appropriate time pointed to the painting
and was silent. Then he said, "Yes, look at this with seriousness and reflection. We will render an account to God—we and all the heads of
state who bear responsibility for the fate of the nations . . . in all conscience let them give ear to the anguished cry of 'Peace, Peace,' which
rises up to Heaven from every part of the world, from innocent children and from those grown old. . . . May this thought of the reckoning
that they are to face spur them to make every effort toward achieving
this blessing which for the human family is a greater blessing than any
other" (from the *Stories of Good Pope John,* p. 39).

Jesus is dying, being murdered, and it's all legal. All the rules were
followed. All the details attended to, religiously and politically, with the

leaders of the nation and the religion all playing their parts according to the rules. This is the way most of the killing is still done in war, individually and on a larger scale: abortion, euthansia, the death penalty, torture within acceptable limits, wars of attrition, for security, for expansion of territory, for prevention, for revenge, for nationalistic fervor, for aggression, and to make a point. The end is the same: death.

Let us pray: Lord, we look upon you, crucified and stretched out between heaven and earth, wide open to attack, yet embracing the world as you are nailed to the wood of the cross. And you pray. You forgive us. You forgive us for all the hate, the murder, the killing and war, the destruction and the seeding of more war and revenge and fear. May we accept your forgiveness and turn and forgive one another, all others who we name enemies, terrorists, or threats to us. And in turn, may we ask forgiveness of those we have gone to war against and harmed. May we stretch out our arms to embrace the world and seek to make peace as you have made peace with us through your blood, your suffering, and your Cross. Amen.

The Eleventh Station

■

JESUS PROMISES
TO SHARE HIS REIGN
WITH THE GOOD THIEF

■

SCRIPTURE: LUKE 23:39–43

One of the criminals hanging in crucifixion blasphemed him: "Aren't you the Messiah? Then save yourself and us." But the other one rebuked him: "Have you no fear of God, seeing you are under the same sentence? We deserve it, after all. We are only paying the price for what we've done, but this man has done nothing wrong." He then said, "Jesus, remember me when you enter upon your reign." And Jesus replied, "I assure you: this day you will be with me in paradise."

■ ■ ■ ■ ■ ■

Are you willing to believe that even though they are guilty of a diabolical act, they still continue to be children of God, not monsters, not demons, but those with the capacity to change?

ARCHBISHOP DESMOND TUTU OF SOUTH AFRICA

There are three criminals hanging on their crosses. We have made the other two thieves, but they are not called thieves. To merit crucifixion the crimes would have been that of murder, sedition, treason against Rome, terrorism—the crimes of Barabbas, who had killed soldiers in an uprising against the state and who was set free instead of Jesus. These are the crimes of the men who share Jesus' dying. All are in agony, suffering terribly. But we know from the Scriptures that Jesus is being mocked, insulted, jeered at, with the soldiers offering him sour wine and taunting him mercilessly. And the two on either side must make a decision whether to just hang there and die, join the others in the mockery and anger, venting their rage on Jesus verbally, or turn toward him. And each chooses.

One blasphemes him, curses him, joining those on the ground in their disgust. But the other seems to watch Jesus' reactions to what has been done to him and to the vehemence all around him and begins to wonder . . . what if he is who he says he is? Jesus' behavior is nonviolent, no matter what is done to him, and this criminal has heard him pray lines from psalms and even ask forgiveness for those who do him evil and take his life. He risks incurring the wrath of the soldiers and others on the ground by speaking to Jesus. He shares his rejection and aligns himself with Jesus. A simple act, a kindness that could turn some of the mockery toward him and make his situation worse. He turns toward the other criminal and rebukes him on Jesus' behalf, saying, "Have you no fear of God, seeing you are under the same sentence? We deserve it, after all. We are only paying the price for what we've done, but this man has done nothing wrong." This is his confession, his humble acceptance of his part in evil and at the same moment he separates Jesus from them, proclaiming his innocence and the truth of who Jesus is. The other had mocked him as a false Messiah, the "anointed one" who would save the people from their sins, because, like the others, he thought that meant from the Romans and their position as slaves in occupied territory.

And then he turns toward Jesus and implores him, "Remember me when you come into your power, your reign, the place where you dwell." Is it faith? Yes, if faith is an action. He puts himself one step lower than where he was, sharing Jesus' place of poverty, insecurity, and the focus of rage. Remember me. And he will be remembered, because of his association with the Crucified One. He will be remembered in word and story and held up as hope for change for everyone, no matter what they have done. Not only does the presence of God suffering in Jesus offer forgiveness to all for anything, it is the doorway to another kind of living and dying, now, here on earth. To remember means to put back together again, as it was meant to be, or was originally. And for this criminal, in his last moments, his life is put back together again, and he is assured of being in the presence of God, in the reign of God, forever.

Earlier in Mark's gospel (10:37) there were two who wanted first seats on either side of Jesus in his kingdom. James and John, the "sons of Thunder," as they were nicknamed, the cousins of Jesus. In fact, in one of the accounts they sent their mother in to ask the favor of Jesus, causing others to become indignant when their action was revealed (Mt. 20:20–27). They were looking out for their future, seeking to guarantee their positions in the kingdom now, and share his glory. Jesus tells them, "You do not know what you are asking. Can you drink the cup I shall drink or be baptized in the same bath as I?" They glibly answer, "We can" (Mk. 10:35–39). He tells them that they will indeed one day drink from the cup and share the baptism but that those seats in the kingdom are not his to give. That prerogative belongs to his Father and it is reserved for others. The reservation belongs to the two criminals that now hang side by side with Jesus crucified and being baptized into this bath of blood and pain.

James and John were ambitious, seeking power, and later Jesus tells all of them that in his kingdom things are very different than in the kingdoms of the world. He declares openly to them, "The Son of Man has not come to be served but to serve—to give his life in ransom for the many" (Mk. 10:45). Access to places of power in his kingdom are awarded and given to those who step down to share the pain of those in a worse position than they are and align themselves with the poorest of the poor, the criminal, the terrorist, those accused of sedition and murder, those we would not want to be associated with in life, let alone die with, under the same sentence.

The hard question of this station is, "Who are we aligning ourselves with?" Are we aligning ourselves with the presence of God as it is abused, broken, bleeding, and mocked and scorned even now in this world? Do we take that one step down, risking insecurity, violence, guilt by association, to stand beside those who are both victim, accused, and public sinner—criminal and despised in society?

Jesus teaches even in death by his very presence and how he conducts himself in brutal, violent circumstances. And Jesus' body, his life, his silence, and his forgiveness call out for a decision: for good or for evil. Presence can be confrontation as surely as words. We never know how our being in any situation will affect those around us, even people we despise, fear, hate, and reject. The lines of Aleksandr Solzhenitsyn, who spent years in the Gulag of Siberia, are ones that we must remember and take heart from, even as the criminal who turned toward Jesus took heart from overheard words.

> The line separating good and evil passes not through states,
> nor between classes, not between political parties either—but
> right through every human heart. . . . This line shifts. Inside
> us, it oscillates with the years. And even within hearts over-
> whelmed with evil, one small bridgehead of good is retained.
> And even in the best of hearts, there remains . . . an unup-
> rooted small corner of evil.

Jesus' message is the good news of forgiveness, conversion, a hope for another life, an alternative to the harm and injustice, sin and evil that we have done before. We are continually being asked to choose. Our second baptismal promise is, "Do you promise to resist evil and refuse to be mastered by any sin?" Any sin? By nationalism, racism, violence that is personal or political or economic? By lying, cheating, stealing, greed, hate, anger, vengeance, selfishness? By support of domestic policies that do not honor the common good of the majority and care for the poor first so that there is equity in the land? By support of international policies that afford a privileged status to our own country while causing injustice elsewhere? By support of death: abortion, capital punishment, euthanasia, military budgets in billions of dollars that cause instability worldwide, plans for newer levels of nuclear weapons that threaten the very existence of humankind and the planet? What we do—individually, in churches, groups, political parties, communities—affects others, and we must remember our presence is always part of the situation, for better or for worse. Fyodor Dostoevsky, the Russian novelist, wrote in *The Brothers Karamazov* lines that bear remembering in his reflection on as examination of our own consciences:

> If the evil-doing of men moves you to indignation and overwhelming distress, even to a desire for vengeance on the evildoers, shun above all things that feeling. Go at once and seek suffering for yourself, as though you were yourself guilty of that wrong. Accept that suffering and bear it and your heart will find comfort, and you will understand that you, too, are guilty, for you might have been a light to the evil-doers, even as the one man sinless, and you were not a light to them. If you had been a light, you would have lightened the path for others too, and the evil-doer might perhaps have been saved by your light from his sin. An even though your light was shining, yet you see men were not saved by it, hold firm and doubt not the power of the heavenly light. Believe that if they were not saved, they will be saved hereafter. And if they are not saved hereafter, then their sons will be saved. . . .

We are all under the same sentence: of living with one another in this world and called to live as humanly as possible, in obedience to the will of God, which is life for everyone. We must learn to be mindful, to remember God is the King of the Universe (though in this station he is declared a criminal and mocked as the King of the Jews, intended as an insult by the Romans). And because of our being bound to honor God, we are bound to one another in Christ Jesus, and we must therefore remember one another in all that we choose to do or not do.

There is an Islamic parable from the Sufi tradition that will help us remember. Once upon a time there was a businessman travelling in another country. He looked for a mosque to attend the daily prayers. The only one he could find was a very poor, decrepit, and worn building on the edge of the warehouse district, nearby the company he was doing business with. He felt a bit awkward, even ashamed, about attending, because his clothing was so much more expensive than those of others who worshipped with him. He thought about it throughout all the prayers and lingered afterwards, allowing the others to leave first. When he arrived outside, he realized his shoes were gone. The man in charge was distressed at seeing that there were no shoes left and the guest was in his stocking feet. He was ashamed: what would he think of the community, that they were all thieves? But the man told him not to worry about it, saying, "It was my fault altogether. I tempted every man who entered to pray, with my shoes. Many had shoes that barely stayed together, and all too many didn't have any shoes at all. Now someone in need has my shoes, and Allah the most Compassionate has relieved me of my pride and insensitivity to those worse off than I am."

Let us pray: Lord Jesus Christ, remember us when you come into your kingdom. Help us to live turning always toward your forgiveness, your truthfulness, and your way of nonviolent response to evil. May your presence among us teach us to honor the presence of all people and remember that the way we conduct ourselves in this world, the way we deal with injustice and sin presents a chance for others to choose life or to choose to side with situations of evil and injustice. Let us never give in to our anger, even in our pain, but remind us to call out to you, confident that you will respond with more help than we could have hoped for. Lord, remember us when you come into your kingdom, now and forever. Amen.

The Twelfth Station

■

JESUS IS ON THE CROSS, WITH HIS MOTHER AND DISCIPLE BELOW

■

SCRIPTURE: JOHN 19:25–27
Near the cross of Jesus there stood his mother, his mother's sister, Mary the wife of Clopas, and Mary Magdalene. Seeing his mother there with the disciple whom he loved, Jesus said to his mother, "Woman, there is your son." In turn he said to the disciple, "There is your mother." From that hour onward, the disciple took her into his care.

Or

SCRIPTURE: LUKE 2:34–35
Simeon blessed them and said to Mary his mother, "This child is destined to be the downfall and the rise of many in Israel, a sign that will be opposed—and you yourself shall be pierced with a sword—so that the thoughts of many hearts may be laid bare.

■　■　■　■　■　■

You may call God love, you may call God goodness.
But the best name for God is compassion.
MEISTER ECKHART

This is a station of tender regard and profound pain. Jesus hangs above, looking down upon those he loves, his relatives and friends. And those who are bound together in their love for him hold each other up, looking up at Jesus crucified, drawing all things upward to himself. Four grieving figures who can do nothing but be there, standing nearby, attend at the deathbed made of hard wood and hate. They stand under the shadow of the cross and the hanging body of Christ. Jesus is dying, and yet he is very aware of others: those whose pain is caused by his own suffering and their love for him. The phrase "seeing his mother there with the disciple whom he loved" seems to say that their presence together is what causes him to speak, to make formal what is already a reality. They are taking care of each other, their arms around each other in their grief. They are each losing the person that is most dear to them, and they are bereft of any comfort.

He speaks to his mother first, calling her "Woman," a title of respect that he has used with other women in the gospel, who show great faith, compassion for others, or enduring grace. And he commands here in formal language, "Behold your son." And then turning to the beloved disciple, he continues in the same manner: "Behold your mother." It is as though this is a court of law and there is an adoption proceeding being confirmed and ritualized for the future, altering the basic relationships of those involved. They are given over to each other, for mutual support, comfort, life and needs shared. They become blood relatives. They are bound now in a new covenant, a new family, with blood ties born of pain, the Way of the Cross, the truth of the gospel and companionship, discipleship in the Lord. They are responsible now for one another, basing their relationship on the one each had shared with Jesus, who has brought them together. She is a widow. The beloved disciple is young, perhaps fifteen years old.

But the "beloved disciple" is not actually named, so tradition tells us that it is not just John who is the "beloved disciple," but by baptism in John's community, every newly baptized Christian, every young Christian is to be the beloved disciple and have the same relationship with Jesus that young John had. They are given the gospel the night of their baptisms, when they are initiated into the death and resurrection of Jesus and therefore live now, no longer for themselves alone, but "hidden with Christ in God" (Col. 3:3). They are given intimacy with Jesus and now, in this passage, responsibility for not only his mother, but all widows and those associated with those condemned to death, who struggle for justice and care for the poor and suffer with Christ because of their closeness to him, their standing near the Cross.

The readings from John and Luke can be tied together. From the beginning the newly baptized person lives under the shadow of the Cross. Signed with it, baptized in water three times in the name of the Trinity, sealed with it with oil, and the trace marking our foreheads, we belong now to God, as expressed by the ancient words of pre-baptism: "You are already saved, but on your knees and under the sign of the cross." This is the connection to the blessing that Mary receives when she and Joseph come to present Jesus their firstborn as a sacrifice belonging to God. Simeon, the old prophet, blesses her with strange words that are about her child and what being connected to him intimately will mean for her and anyone who is born of water and the spirit. "This child is destined to be the downfall and the rise of many in Israel, a sign that will be opposed." This is an apt description of what this child dedicated to the will of God has grown up to be, a sign lifted up, a contradiction, the cause of division and life-and-death choices. And because of this, she is told "and you yourself shall be pierced with a sword—so that the thoughts of many hearts may be laid bare" (Lk. 2:34–35). This sword has always been a way of describing the Word of God, the double-edged sword that cuts to the heart, clean down to bone, causing us to be seen and known for what we truly are at our roots (Heb. 4:12). As disciples we, like Mary, the "beloved disciple," and the other two Marys, have always stood under the sign of the cross, living in its shadow, and have always been given the Word of the Lord, the Scriptures, as our only sword of power and insight. It lays us bare, and in our response and obedience to it, it lays bare the hearts of those around us and in relationship to us.

There is an old saying that blood is thicker than water. Not so in Jesus' new family, in his kingdom. The waters of baptism override any familial ties. If there are blood ties, it is not those of family heritage and ancestral trees, but the blood of the Cross—the tree soaked with the blood of Christ, in death and in the Eucharist. This is the station of compassion, of the drawing together of the new family of Jesus, given to one another to care for each other as tenderly as we would for Jesus, Jesus' mother, and those who are closest to them and so closest to us. All of these people are poor, the women and mothers who lose their children to violence, to state-sanctioned terrorism, to torture, and to unjust systems of collusion between religious bodies, economic groups, and nations. We must stand with them as prophets, advocates, speaking out on behalf of those without rights in society: widows, orphans, criminals, those in occupied territories, struggling for freedom as children of God, those who opposed injustice and live by the corporal works of mercy, feeding the hungry and giving them shelter, caring for the sick, setting the prisoners free, and burying the dead. We stand with them at the foot of the cross, looking upon the Crucified One, the beloved of our lives, given to each other by him, and knowing our hearts will be pierced so that the hearts of others might come to belief. They are to watch us and see through us to the truth of Jesus' message of the kingdom, the children of God.

Often in the gospels we are told the story of Jesus with his disciples and people coming in to tell him that his mother, his brothers, sisters, blood family, and relations are outside and waiting for him. But he does not go out to them. Instead he is very clear in saying who is tied to him by blood and water and love. "Who are my mother and my brothers?" And gazing around him at those seated in the circle, he continues: "These are my mother and my brothers. Whoever does the will of my Father is brother and sister and mother to me" (Mk 3:31–35).

And again, when he hears his mother blessed for bearing him, he says, "Rather blessed are they who hear the word of God and keep it" (Lk.11:27–28).

Jesus' family are those who share his terrible darkness, who pick up their cross and come after him and bear one another's burdens. We are the mothers and sisters and brothers of Jesus, obedient to his Word and his Father, intent on giving the tender regard and compassion of Jesus that he showed for his own mother and friends to all those around us. And we find them near the cross, under its shadow, sometimes beckoning though more often than not silent, wrapped in grief, burdened by unbearable loss and knowing that they will go home alone, widowed, orphaned, belonging to no one. These are the ones we are given to and who are given to us in this ritual of making family at the foot of the cross. All of us are passionately attached to our friends and those who share our dreams just as those who stood at the foot of the cross were passionately attached to Jesus: his mother, the beloved disciple, his mother's sister, and Mary of Magdala. But we are being called to a new and deeper passion: to those who live under the shadow of the cross and those most in need of compassion. Then we become mothers of God, sisters and brothers of Jesus, beloved disciples born in the blood of the Cross and fed on the Word of God. This is our greatest blessing, the one that comes from intimacy with those who suffer with the broken and hanging body of our God. We are a family born of grief, united in Christ, sharing our sorrow.

Just after the Peace Accords were signed in Northern Ireland there was a bomb explosion in a crowded shopping area in Omagh. A young girl, Julie Miller, wrote a song called "Broken Things," inspired by the biblical message that the Lord is close to the broken-hearted and those crushed in spirit.

You can have my heart if you don't mind broken things;
You can have my life if you don't mind these tears:
Well, I heard that you make old things new

So I give these pieces all to you
If you want it you can have my heart.

Father Kevin Mullan, eloquently summed up the people's feelings in
Omagh this way:

> At this hour last Saturday 28 good and deeply loved people,
> one carrying twins awaiting birth, were alive in these streets.
> Each of them, each of us, at this hour last Saturday had a fu-
> ture for some time on this earth. But the future had already
> been brought among us. Evil had already possessed some hu-
> man hearts and minds to do evil unto human beings. At 10
> minutes past 3 on August 15 the future came. Death and life
> were blasted together. Death carried life and peace away. It
> searched for many more of us with its savage scorching breath.
> Its bloody greed was fought in the street and the hospital by
> those who love and treasure life and dearly loved the lives for
> whom they fought. Now both sides are united in grief. But our
> private sorrow can only last so long. Life goes on. In screams
> or peals of laughter, but it hurts.
>
> (FROM A NEWSPAPER CLIPPING)

The Crucifixion continues. The grieving is fresh, as fresh as the blood
spilled. But life goes on, and for us who are the children of God, life
goes on under the shadow of the cross, with a new family to hold on to
us, their arms around us, and we are exhorted to take care of the left-
overs, the victims, the ones who are broken and bent, the ones who are
scarred and will remember forever.

Let us pray: Oh God, we stand beneath your cross, with Mary our
Mother. We stand as disciples and friends devoted to you and all those
who know the pain of hatred and the suffering inflicted upon them by
injustice and evil. And we vow to stop the pain. We vow to ease the
grief. We vow to stand with the condemned and the victims until we

make such horrors as the death penalty, executions, terrorism, and legally sanctioned killing unthinkable. We vow to uncrucify, to take down those hanged in hatred, and to oppose those who crucify still. Hold us to our word, for it is yours. Feed us on your Word, and may the only sword we ever wield be the double-edged sword of truth that is used to fight with justice and mercy, out of compassion for others. May we look upon all those in such need with compassion, as you ever look upon us. Amen.

The Thirteenth Station

■

JESUS DIES
ON THE
CROSS

■

SCRIPTURE: MATTHEW 27:45–50

From noon onward, there was darkness over the whole land until midafternoon. Then toward midafternoon Jesus cried out in a loud tone, "Eli, Eli, lama sabachthani," that is, "My God, my God, why have you forsaken me?" This made some of the bystanders who heard it remark, "He is invoking Elijah!" Immediately one of them ran off and got a sponge. He soaked it in cheap wine, and sticking it on a reed, tried to make him drink. Meanwhile the rest said, "Leave him alone. Let us see whether Elijah comes to his rescue." Once again Jesus cried out in a loud voice, and then gave up his spirit.

Or

SCRIPTURE: MARK 15:33–37

When noon came, darkness fell on the whole countryside and lasted until midafternoon. At that time Jesus cried in a loud voice, "Eloi, Eloi, lama sabachthani?" which means, "My God, my God, why have you forsaken me?" A few of the bystanders who heard it remarked, "Listen! He is calling on Elijah!" Someone ran off, and soaking a sponge in sour wine, stuck it on a reed to try to make him drink. The man said, "Now let's see whether Elijah comes to take him down." Then Jesus, uttering a loud cry, breathed his last.

■ ■ ■ ■ ■ ■

You have been appointed
to ask mercy for the world,
to keep vigil
for the salvation of all,
and to partake in
every means of suffering,
both of the just and
the sinners.

—ISAAC THE SYRIAN

Ave Crux, spes unica.
Hail Cross, our only hope.

—MOTTO OF ST. EDITH STEIN (SR. TERESIA BENEDICTA OF THE CROSS,
PHILOSOPHER, MARTYR, CARMELITE)

Jesus dies. But he dies by crying out in a loud voice. How do we let go of life, especially when that life so cherished is torn from you in violence, before its fulfillment? Jesus dies, at the rough hands of others. He dies slowly, and as he draws near to the end he prays, crying aloud to God. His cry is misunderstood. They think he's calling on Elijah the prophet, and they try, by giving him crude wine, to delay his actual death. They just want to see if his prayer will be answered, if Elijah will come to rescue him. Still they treat him crassly, as though he was something to observe, with no care for his suffering and who he is, even as he dies. But Jesus is praying one of the psalms, crying out in agony, and sheer human bodily need for deliverance, for endurance, for some shred of humanness in this nightmarish last few moments of his life. Here is where his pain-racked body and his utter failure in obeying his beloved Father's command to bring the kingdom of good news, of justice with peace to the earth, and the utter aloneness that every human faces dying come together.

His suffering is abhorrent and it is ignored. Yet Jesus dies, as the Suffering Servant of Yahweh, overcoming evil with good, embracing death, as he does his enemies, with love. Jesus prays Psalm 22. It is a psalm of desperate need and trust in God in the midst of brutal inhumanity borne in one's flesh. For twenty lines it is a litany of pain, of what he feels, of what has been done to his body. And then it turns, toward hope, belief, and utter purity of worship and belonging to God alone. It carries lines like these!

> *So by your gift will I utter praise in the vast assembly;*
> *I will fulfill my vows before those who fear him.*
> *The lowly shall eat their fill; they who seek the Lord shall praise him;*
> *"May your hearts be ever merry!"*
>
> (v. 25–27)

> *For dominion is the Lord's, and he rules the nations.*
> *To him alone shall bow down all who sleep in the earth; . . .*

and to him my soul shall live; my descendants shall serve him.
Let the coming generations be told of the Lord that they may proclaim
to a people yet to be born the justice he has shown.

(v. 28–31)

Jesus dies, but he lays down his life; it is not taken from him. Jesus dies, but he puts his life and his spirit into the hands of God, praising his justice and fulfilling his vows and repeating the truth that God is the only power in heaven and on earth and to God alone will all those who live and die bow down. His dying, as his living, will be an act of faith and unfailing love for his beloved God Father.

This is a battle between all the power of evil and all the power of goodness. Jesus is drawing all things to himself as he is lifted up in crucifixion and death. Moses lifted up the serpent wrapped around the staff and called the people to look upon it and be healed (Nu. 21:4–9). In John's gospel Jesus says, "When you lift up the Son of Man, you will come to realize that I AM and that I do nothing by myself. I say only what the Father has taught me. The One who sent me is with me. He has not deserted me since I always do what pleases him" (Jn. 8:28–29). And lastly he preaches, "Now has judgment come upon this world, now will this world's prince be driven out, and I—once I am lifted up from earth—will draw all to myself" (Jn. 12:31–32). Jesus' death is for the healing for the nations, for wisdom and knowledge of God and for vanquishing the powers of evil and sin in the world. This is paradoxically Jesus' hour of glory and his hour of emptying out all that he is in love and in mercy, for us—for all of us, enemies and friends, pulled together into the unity of God. This is life and death that is filled with grace and power for those who have the eyes to see and the ears to hear what is happening. The impossible is happening—God is dying with us and for us and into us so that we will live and not die the death of sin and evil. It is a moment of impossible choices and impossible graces. This is a way to describe what is happening in words from another tradition:

Things undreamt of are daily being seen, the impossible is ever
becoming possible. We are constantly being astonished these
days at the amazing discoveries in the field of violence. But I
maintain that far more undreamt of and seemingly impossible
discoveries will be made in the field of nonviolence.

(MAHATMA GANDHI)

Jesus, in a sense, grabs hold of his death and dies it for the love of
all people—those who inflicted such viciousness upon him, those who
didn't notice much, those he had healed and were now nowhere to be
seen, those who ran and betrayed him, and those who stayed, nearby or
at a distance, and us, wherever we chose to be, at the moment that cry
pierces the veil between heaven and earth.

Jesus dies with a loud cry. There is a book called *Cry of Jesus, Cry
of the Oppressed,* by José Comblin (out of print, N.Y., Orbis) that
speaks about that cry. What is that cry? What does it reveal? What does
it scream into the very air of the universe? Following is a piece that
takes ideas from that book plus from many communities' prayers in
South America in the decades since the 1980s, in trying to say what
the cry is and what happens when you hear it and it pierces your soul
and wounds you in your heart.

Then Jesus cries out.
It is a cry of freedom. A cry of hope. A cry of handing over.
*It is a cry of giving back. Giving back all his work, his dreams, his
    love, life, breath, spirit.*
It is a cry of pain and agony. It is a cry of resistance to evil.
It is a cry against violence and death.
It is a cry that rends the curtain of the temple in two,
    and tears the light out of the day and throws him clear of hate.
It is a cry that throws him into the arms of Mercy.
It is his death cry and it is the beginning of resurrection.

That cry tears loose anything that holds back God or the kingdom
    of God from coming among us.
It is a cry for the poor, for those who struggle for justice and
    for those who hang on for a dearer life,
    for those who hunger and thirst for God's reign, now, in history.
It is a cry for an alternative to injustice, to despair and inhumanity.
A cry that creates a new world like the original one was intended.
It is a cry of judgment and nothing will ever be the same again.
It is the cry of all human beings caught in death,
    caught in a world turning on itself and eating each other alive.
It is a cry layered and fraught with meaning.
It is a cry of prayer to God for justice, for security, for defense and
    for faithfulness that will not be undone by others' hate and
    persecution.
It is a cry of anguish for all that was lost, for all that life that was
    torn to shreds,
    all that life denied to others, all that hope cast away.
All that life that was buried under greed.
All that life that was
    never allowed to blossom, to grow, to thrive and generate new
    life.
It is the Cry of Mercy being poured out
    and Mercy being caught up into the arms of the Father.
It is the Cry of God when we don't see Him.

Jesus dies, and something happens, and the world will never be the same again. It is the tradition of the early church that with this cry, the world went into reverse! Everything since the beginning, all the choices for evil, all the choices against peace, against communion and unity, against good and kindness, turned and went into reverse! The world begins to return to God, and the first ones to turn are the poor, and those who sought justice, who spoke the truth and stood up for others' rights and cared for the needs and wounds of the victims. That cry reverberates throughout history, throughout all time, and is in the very air we breathe, in the Scriptures and liturgy, in the Eucharist, and in the community of believers.

And when we hear that cry, our world begins to go into reverse, and we turn. We turn all our decisions, our choices toward God and God's hope for life on earth. We put in reverse what has destroyed and served evil, and we become undone. The Stations of the Cross, this devotion, leads us steadily, faithfully, unrelentingly to this moment and this cry from the cross. We stand here, waiting for Jesus to cry out. Waiting for him to hand over his life. This is the God of life, who cherishes all life and sent his beloved child into the world for life, life ever more abundantly for all (Jn. 10:10), and he lets go, and it goes forth from him in a great cry. It is meant to shatter our minds, pierce our hearts, and lay bare our souls, turning us toward God, turning us toward Peace, turning us toward community and home.

Now it is time for us to die. Time to be stilled and quieted. Time to listen to the stillness after the cry and let the Spirit of the Crucified One speak to us. And then, with Jesus, it is time to die, to gather our life, to gather all that we hold dear and give it back to the One who made us. "Father, into your hands I give my spirit."

And then there is silence. Jesus is dead.

Let us pray: Father, Jesus handed over his life to your waiting heart. But he had belonged to you from the very first moment. He loved and cherished all life that you had made, and especially he held dear the lives of those who to the rest of the world were expendable, thought of as collateral damage or just statistics, the thousands or the millions. Father, we love the life you have given to us and share with us ever more deeply in Jesus the Lord. May we honor all life and handle it carefully. May we pray daily with Jesus the intention of giving back to you all that you have given to us, our very selves and our life. Father, into your hands I give my spirit. Take us, Oh loving Father, all of us, and hold us to your heart. Amen.

The Fourteenth Station

■

JESUS
IS PLACED
IN THE TOMB

■

SCRIPTURE: MATTHEW 27:57–61

When evening fell, a wealthy man from Arimathaea arrived, Joseph by name. He was another of Jesus' disciples, and had gone to request the body of Jesus. Thereupon Pilate issued an order for its release. Taking the body, Joseph wrapped it in fresh linen and laid it in his own new tomb which had been hewn from a formation of rock. Then he rolled a huge stone across the entrance of the tomb and went away. But Mary Magdalene and the other Mary remained sitting there, facing the tomb.

Or

SCRIPTURE: MARK 15:46

Then, having brought a linen shroud, Joseph took him down, wrapped him in the linen, and laid him in a tomb which had been cut out of rock. Finally he rolled a stone across the entrance of the tomb.

■　■　■　■　■

The world is God's body. God draws it ever upwards.

PIERRE TEILHARD DE CHARDIN

People usually consider walking on water or in thin air a miracle. But I think the real miracle is . . . to walk the earth.

THICH NHAT HANH

Jesus is buried. He is carefully, though hastily, laid in a tomb hewn out of a rock formation. The earth takes back its maker. The preparations are that of any burial except that there are details to settle with the state. There must be a formal request, an investigation, to ascertain whether or not the criminal is actually dead, and then a release for the body. Paperwork, and then the sense that it's over and done with. A stone seals the entrance to the tomb. There is a silence to this station. After the reading it seems to pervade and seep through the air, into your bones. It is the silence of afterwards. It is the silence of the earth, of ages, of rock formations, of canyon walls, and of rings in ancient trees. It is the silence of underground, of waterways and layers of sediment and cores of minerals, strata of the creation.

And then it is night and darkness descends, and everyone goes about their duties. The two Marys eventually get up and go back to where they are staying; and it is the Sabbath, and there is much to attend to on the Sabbath, the day that belongs to God alone, there are no other details allowed. And then in the night another silence comes. It is the silence of the vast heavens, the stars and the planets. The silence of time passing—again, of ages upon ages in the universe. The God who became human, became flesh and blood, became mortal, is dead, killed at the hands of anger and hate, fear and rejection. The world is hushed. If anything is to be said, it can barely be above a whisper. Earth and air, water and the fires of the sky are reverent and still. The body of the beloved of the Father, the maker and keeper of all things, lies in the womb of Mother the Earth. The flesh of the Son of Justice rests at long last in stone. Father the Sky carries the lingering traces of his last loud cry as the sky carries the trace of birds flying across its face.

But though it is quiet, nothing is sleeping. All is awaiting the coming of the fullness of justice, of peace and mercy, the fullness of the power of God. The universe, all of creation, breathes and hums as it holds in its womb the body of Jesus. In John's gospel we find these words:

The hour has come for the Son of Man to be glorified. I
solemnly assure you, unless the grain of wheat falls to the
earth and dies, it remains just a grain of wheat. But if it dies, it
produces much fruit.

(JN. 12:23B–24)

The seed of life, of hope, of justice and mercy, lies buried, but the hour
is coming, the hour of glory when much fruit is produced. Jesus' flesh
is taking root, and will become transformed into light that will shatter
this night and alter forever the course of the universe and its inhabitants. All of creation will know the touch of the God of incarnation,
life, death, and soon, resurrection. The maturation, the transfiguring,
the hope is gathering and growing. What will happen follows the pattern of the Creator, who seeded ways in the universe from the beginning. Listen to the wonder!

The sun, each second, transforms 4 million tons of itself into
light. . . . Human generosity is possible only because at the
center of the solar system a magnificent stellar generosity
pours forth free energy day and night without stop and without
complaint and without the slightest hesitation.

(BRIAN SWIMME)

And here sleeps the Sun of Justice, the Day Star, the Light of the
World! This is the station of the universe and its endless silence. It
seems only recently that we have become aware that our behaviors and
patterns of living are creating havoc within the solar system and on the
earth itself, rendering whole species extinct and putting thousands
more, daily, on the endangered list. We are killing the marvelous things
around us in a frenzy of feeding off natural resources, an addiction to
oil and gas when there are other energy sources available that are end-
lessly renewable, like wind and solar power. This greed to possess and
make the earth serve a small minority's limitless capacity to devour ex-

tends to our food and water supplies. Companies artifically produce seed strains of rice, potatoes, corn, and wheat that do not reseed themselves so that patents must be repurchased yearly, and at the same time they destroy the ancient varieties of crops that are packed with nutrition and taste so that entire peoples can base their diet upon them.

We use chemicals and artifically manufactured biological sprays, additives, and compounds to speed up growth and alter shape and size while changing the innate characteristics of many plants, vegetables, trees, and even species of fish like salmon and shrimp, destroying millennium-based gene pools and resources that have fed the human family and provided richness and variety in the face of drought and other weather disasters.

And now even what we can see in the night sky is impeded. In 1955 Ray Bradbury, a science-fiction writer, wrote a children's book called *Switch on the Night*. It was a touching tale of a lonely young boy who was afraid of the dark and not only wouldn't go outside at night but didn't even use light switches—they seemed somehow dangerous— to turn off the lights inside, so he kept all the house lights on, day and night. One night late he is visited by a young girl named Dark who teaches him a wonder: that you can turn on and off the Night, just like you can the lights in your house! She shows him, turning off all the lights, and there in every window of the house are the lights of the night: the stars! She calls them "the light stars, the bright stars, the true stars, the blue stars." We are being warned that most of us today don't ever see the stars at night, that the Milky Way can't be seen by two-thirds of the world's population because of severe light pollution. Here's what Les Line says in *Audubon Magazine* (January–February, 2002):

> Whole generations of kids in cities and suburbs are growing up
> seldom if ever having seen what a sky full of thousands of stars
> might look like," says Timothy Ferris, author of best-selling
> books on the cosmos. It could be a big loss, we're told, be-
> cause young skywatchers are the ones who grow up to be po-

ets, philosphers, explorers and scientists. The stars, of course, are still burning bright. They're just waiting for grown-ups to switch on the Night.

(P. 96, IN COLUMN CALLED "ONEPICTURE")

Wendell Berry, theologian and lover of the universe, writes about ecology and our responsibility to the world that God has made and entrusted to us to care for and hand on to those who come after us, down to the seventh generation, as our indigenous people exhort us. He says, "To live we must daily break the body and shed the blood of creation. When we do this knowingly, lovingly, skillfully, reverently, it is a sacrament. When we do it ignorantly, greedily, clumsily, destructively, it is a desecration. In such desecration we condemn ourselves to spiritual and moral loneliness and others to want." With the burial of Jesus, earth itself held onto Hope enfleshed, and even dead Jesus' body brings life, genesis, and new bursts of creation and vitality to the universe that will wait in hope for the fullness of Jesus' resurrection to seep through it and transform it utterly into the kingdom of justice with peace for all that Jesus' presence on the earth began.

A remarkable woman, Terry Tempest Williams of Utah, who has lived through and chronicled her family's loss of life to cancer based on environmental destruction, writes passionately of the earth and our future together on it. She speaks of the earth, specifically where she lives, outside Salt Lake City, Utah, but of all creation in terms of family, of new creation and hope for our children and our childrens' children down to the seventh generations:

> Would you believe me when I tell you this is my family, kinship with the desert, the breadth of my relations coursing through a wider community, the shock of recognition with each scarlet gila, the smell of rain. . . . is not the tissue of family always a movement between harmony and distance?

Perhaps it is time to give birth to a new idea, many new ideas. Perhaps it is time to give birth to new institutions, to overhaul our religious, political, legal and educational systems that are no longer working for us. Perhaps it is time to adopt a much needed code of ethics, one that will exchange the sacred rights of humans for the rights of all beings on the planet.

We can begin to live differently.

We have choices before us, conscious choices, choices of conscience and consequence, not in the name of political correctness, but ecological responsibility and opportunity.

We give birth to creation.

To labor in the name of social change. To bear down and push against the constraints of our self-imposed structures. To sacrifice in the name of an ecological imperative. To be broken open to a new way of being.

(TERRY TEMPEST WILLIAMS, EXCERPTED FROM THE ESSAY

"LABOR" IN *RED* [NEW YORK: RANDOM HOUSE, 2001].)

Earth was Jesus' tomb. What if in the paradoxically wondrous way of God's transformation and resurrection of Jesus, earth was Jesus' womb? And what if God is ultimately concerned with all the life that is in his womb, the universe and all the myriad species of life created on this planet? What if earth is not only our home, our dwelling place, the place where the kingdom of God comes in its wholeness, now, in history, but what if earth too is part of our family, redeemed and transfigured by the body and blood of Christ, who walked upon it and loved its rivers and hills and seas and cities and the vast wild places he went to pray in? What if Jesus' unbearable compassion and vast kindness extends to all that was made before we arrived on the last day?

The two Marys sit and face the tomb, watching. They know their Lord and Love lies within. Now they think he will return to the earth, to dust, his bones and flesh disintegrating, disappearing to be food for the earth as are all human beings. He is dead and buried. Earth holds on to Jesus' body very carefully, as carefully as we are to tread on and use the earth, because earth will not be able to hold on to Jesus' body when the Father bends down to kiss life back into his beloved child. And we are not to hold on to the earth, waters, sky, and air—the universe—as if it were ours. Like Jesus' visit to the womb of earth that held him as a mother holds her child, we are to tend to this mother that bears us on her back and this father that feeds us air—that one day we too will give back to God.

In the Orthodox tradition late in the services of Good Friday the body of Jesus is carried through the church and then covered with a platnykta, an elaborate and finely woven burial shroud. Later, when these cloths have grown worn and thin from long use, they are given to members of the community and are hung in guest bedrooms. I used to visit someone who had one of these ancient treasures, and I slept under it while there. These are the thoughts suggested for those who sleep under a platnykta, in memory of the Christ who now sleeps in his burial shroud in the tomb.

This borrowed bed in a guest room is not ordinary. My friend is Ruthinian Orthodox, and I sleep under a platnykta. The figure of Jesus laid out for burial, embroidered in fine colors and small stitches lovingly by an old woman's reverent eye and hand, hangs over me. I used to think, looking up at it through the night shadows, that it brooded there, but soon I came to know its comforting presence. It was the comfort of sleeping close beneath the dead God-man whose body was just resting—mourned for, lost, yearned for—just before his Father reached down to touch him and raise him up. Oftentimes now I lie in bed, miles away, looking in my memory for that body's nearness, that Father's tenderness, my life clinging in belief to such power. I stake my life and my long sleep when it comes on such a hope as the old woman's woven into that piece of cloth.

We all live in Christ, and one day we will sleep in Christ and rise in him. It is still all we know and stake our lives on.

Let us pray: Jesus, your body lies inert, bloodied and torn, shredded to pieces, as we often treat the earth we live on and its resources and very air we breathe and water we drink. Joseph, named after the dreamers, takes you down, wraps you in clean linen, washing your body with reverence and devotion. Teach us to honor all that you have made, your earth and sky, water and air, as we are to honor all your children that dwell on this planet turning in this universe. May our minds and our hearts stretch to be able to see your grace and life transforming everything that you have created and loved. May we be as careful with earth as we are commanded to be with the bodies of all your children—as we would be with your body. Amen.

The Fifteenth Station

■

HOLY SATURDAY
AND
EASTER RESURRECTION

■

SCRIPTURE: LUKE 24:1–3

On the first day of the week, at dawn, the women came to the tomb bringing the spices they had prepared. They found the stone rolled back from the tomb, but when they entered the tomb, they did not find the body of the Lord Jesus.

Or

SCRIPTURE: REVELATION 5:12; 7:9–10, 13–14

This is the new hymn they sang: "Worthy is the Lamb that was slain to receive power and riches, wisdom and strength, honor and glory and praise!"

After this I saw before me a huge crowd which no one could count from every nation and race, people and tongue. They stood before the throne of the Lamb, dressed in long white robes and holding palm branches in their hands. They cried out in a loud voice, "Salvation is from our God, who is seated on the throne, and from the Lamb!" . . . Then one of the elders asked me, "Who are these people all dressed in white? And where have they come from?" I said to him, "Sir, you should know better than I." He then told me, "These are the ones who have survived the great period of trial; they have washed their robes and made them white in the blood of the Lamb."

■ ■ ■ ■ ■ ■

Love is the person of the resurrection,
scooping up the dust and chanting, Live.
EMILY DICKINSON

Again there is silence, a space in between what was and what is yet to
be, the unknown and the mystery that is to come. It is the silence before an earthquake, when everything trembles sensing the power that is
coming and how all will be upheaval and opening. It is the silence before a tsunami wave comes over the sea, gathering all the water into its
embrace, racing to the shore all at once. It is the silence before a tor-
nado roars into view, picking up everything in its wake. It is the day we
call Holy Saturday, the night of the vigil that Christians observe as the
critical mass and core of their religion. Jesus has been buried, but his
words linger in hearts half-dead, half-hoping for their truth. "I am the
resurrection and the life, whoever believes in me will never die and
whoever dies will come to life again." (Jn. 11:25)

The vigil begins with an outdoor fire and the blessing of a tall candle that symbolizes the light of Christ, the Risen One, being brought in
honor and rejoicing into a darkened church. We step over the threshold
into the church and into the ritual of making new Christians, those being birthed into the rising of Jesus from the dead. And then it is a long
night of stories, starting in Genesis, when the world and all its wonders
where created and the Holy One found that it was all good. Then stories follow of a people chosen by God and made his own, Abraham and
Isaac, the mighty parting of the waters in the Exodus, the call of the
prophets back again and again to this covenant of life, for the poor, for
justice and peace, for the people to become a light to the other nations.
The stories build until the proclamation is made of who we are in
Christ, buried with Christ in the waters of baptism as he was buried in
the tomb of rock. We are told that "we live now no longer for ourselves
alone, but we live hidden with Christ in God." (Col. 3:3) As the people
were led through the waters of the sea into a promised land, now we
are led through the waters of baptism into the new life of resurrection
and the community of the Trinity.

The utterly unexpected happens because the utterly unbelievable
happened after Jesus was wrapped in his linen shroud and sealed in a
tomb. Jesus was raised from the dead! The seed buried burst through

the ground and opened up. There is now only an empty tomb, a hollowed-out space in a rock. There is no body! This mystery of empti-ness must be entered into and probed deeply, and then we must go forth from our tombs, and from our baptisms, to meet the Risen Crucified One out walking in the world, waiting for us to catch up with him, walk-ing the roads in and out of Jerusalem and on all the roads of the world.

What was dead is alive and is now an altogether different form of life than what was before. And we who are buried with Christ in God know this life now, practice this life until our deaths, and stake our lives on the belief that one day we will all know this resurrection life in fullness, all human beings and the earth itself. That seed bore the fruit of life, of hope and justice, of love and forgiveness, of compassion and mercy for all, but first for those who were ground down and cut down by others. In this blood of martyrs is the seed of Christians. And in the blood of those suffering today there is the family of humankind born in the resurrection of Jesus. And we must die with Christ, again and again, ritually in the week we call Holy, on a Good Friday, and lie in the tomb with Christ on Holy Saturday, waiting for the Father to reach down once again to raise us up as a harvest of justice and peace for the whole world. We are to be balm to soothe the wounds of those who suffer unjustly, a presence with those who are publicly denied life and killed, words of truth to those who continue to force a cross of destruc-tion on others and mock those who follow their Master Jesus in nonvio-lence and loving compassion along the Way of the Cross, all the way to Resurrection's glory.

This Jesus that was lifted up to draw all peoples to himself is now lifted up by his Father. We will honor him in lifting high the cross, which leads us into the church, and by lifting high the Paschal candle newly lit and incensed, which symbolizes the Body of Christ. We will lift high the Scriptures, the Word of God proclaimed as a living pres-ence among us once again and we will lift our hearts in praise and song before our God of Life. We will lift the bread and wine, the Body and Blood of Christ, in a toast of resurrection glory and delight, believing that our God the Father, in the power of the Holy Spirit, will lift us along with Jesus to the fullness of life one day.

But it is silence before and even silence after . . . the tomb is empty and God walks the world. There is darkness ahead, but now there is always another reality, no matter what we must face, no matter what people do to one another or to the earth. We are the people of God, the people of resurrection, and the children of light. We cannot forget, and we must remind one another of, the calling and our being signed with the power of the Cross. We must encourage one another in preaching, in poetry, in music and prayer, in the corporal works of mercy and the insistence on justice for all, beginning with the largest majority in the greatest need. We must dance it, crawl it, and dig it out of the ground, empty the tombs and take down the bodies from the crosses with our bare hands. The power of love unto death, and life beyond death, has been given to us in Resurrection and in our baptisms.

> Difficult and painful as it is, we must walk on in the days
> ahead with an audacious faith in the future. When our days
> become dreary with low-hovering clouds of despair, and when
> our nights become darker than a thousand midnights, let us re-
> member that there is a creative force in this universe, working
> to pull down the gigantic mountains of evil; a power that is
> able to make a way out of no way and transform dark yester-
> days into bright tomorrows.
>
> (MARTIN LUTHER KING, JR.)

With the walking of the Way of the Cross we may feel like we have been stretched to our very limits. Our hearts and minds, our feelings and souls, our decision making and our bodies are stretched. But it is only practice for the stretching beyond limits that Resurrection introduces into the world. Our images of God now must tend toward the lowly, the torn apart and bent double, those nameless and anonymous once living, counted in war as collateral damage, the faces with the eyes like gaping tombs questioning us in photographs, the statistics of government reports representing people who should be off welfare by now, the number of immigrants and strangers detained without cause or representation, the meek—meaning nonviolent people protesting in the streets about world banks, tariffs, quotas, and criteria for loans in a globalized economy that still is based on greed, not the possibility of living for the majority. Our images of God must now bear scars and bloody wounds, bones sticking out, faces that are dark, seamed, and wrinkled from exposure to the elements.

And those who would wear those white garments, baptismal garments washed in the blood of the Lamb, must know that the struggle of being born into this new place is about blood and guts and screaming and crying out and then collapsing in spasms of exhaustion, laughter, tears running down your face, and eyes shining as new life enters the world. For now, nothing is as it seems to be. Nothing is over even when it obviously is. In reality it's just beginning; reality is unraveling, and the mystery is moving in on us. The last lines of the ancient Easter Sermon of St. John Chrysostom puts it all succinctly:

> *Poor death, where is your sting?*
> *Poor hell, where is your triumph?*
> *Christ steps out of the tomb and you are reduced to nothing.*
> *Christ rises and the angels are wild with delight.*
> *Christ rises and life is set free.*
> *Christ rises and the graves are emptied of dead.*
> *Oh, yes, for he broke from the tomb like a flower, a beautiful fruit:*
> *The first fruit of those already gone.*
> *All glory be his, all success and power. . . . for ever and ever. Amen.*
>
> (NEW TRANSLATION BY PAUL ROCHE, *AMERICA*, APRIL 5, 1980.)

Now the only things left in the tomb, buried there where they belong, are hate, inhumanity, injustice, war, killing, starvation, oppression, greed, overweening power, violence, rage and rape, destruction of the earth, despair, and death itself! It is time to seal the tomb again, with all of that debris and garbage inside. They have been stricken, struck with a mortal blow, and they are defanged and undone. Those who have been buried in Christ know! The world and time and all created by God are eastering and rising up to new life again. The universe and all of us are the result of unbearable tenderness, and we are laced and threaded with everlasting life that cannot and will not ever be undone. Hope surrounds and delight stalks our every step, because Love still reigns and seeks us out no matter where we hide or live.

"This is the day the Lord has made" is the refrain we sing for seven weeks of Easter glory. This is the day, and it is every day, because the Crucified One opened his eyes to the incomparable glory of this day after the gloom and gore of what came before. We walk out of the tomb and back into our homes and churches, our workplaces and the weary world, but now we walk the Way of the Cross together with our Crucified and Risen Lord, and we walk all the way with God, all the way to glory.

Let us pray with all those who have believed and have gone before us in faith, and with all the living, especially those who treasure their life but will not cling to it if others seek to break its grace or take life from others. Let us pray with all the angels and all who will come after us because we have believed or in spite of our lack of faith and work for justice. Oh Lord, you alone are worthy of all glory, honor, and praise. You alone, who was crucified and died that we might know how to live and die with truthfulness, are worthy of our worship and devotion. Lay claim to our lives, call us your children, and expect us to be your friends. As you spread your arms out on the cross, embrace us all. May we stand in this image of the sign of the cross, arms outstretched, seeking to hold on to one another, until the day comes when you return to bring us the fullness of life. In the meantime may we seek your crucified face and be found wherever you would have been in the world. In the name of the Father and of the Son and of the Holy Spirit, forever and ever. Amen. Alleluia. He is Risen.

Courtesy of the author

MEGAN MCKENNA is an internationally known author, lecturer, retreat leader, and spiritual director. She received her doctorate from the Graduate Theological Union in Berkeley, California, and has taught and worked in India, Singapore, the Philippines (East Asian Pastoral Institute in Manila), Maryknoll Mission Institutes in New York, Chicago, San Francisco, Dublin, and Albuquerque, New Mexico, where she currently lives. In 2001, Megan McKenna was made an Ambassador of Peace by Pax Christi USA. She is the author of more than fifteen books, including *Send My Roots Rain,* published by Doubleday.